Hitchhiking Home
from Danang

Hitchhiking Home from Danang

A Memoir of Vietnam, PTSD and Reclamation

GERALD A. MCCARTHY

McFarland & Company, Inc., Publishers
Jefferson, North Carolina

ISBN (print) 978-1-4766-9284-5
ISBN (ebook) 978-1-4766-5044-9

Library of Congress and British Library cataloguing data are available

Library of Congress Control Number 2023048850

© 2024 Gerald A. McCarthy. All rights reserved

No part of this book may be reproduced or transmitted in any form or by any means, electronic or mechanical, including photocopying or recording, or by any information storage and retrieval system, without permission in writing from the publisher.

Front cover image: PFC Gerald A. McCarthy, Chu Lai, 1st Engineer Battalion, fall 1966; *background* © LNLong/Shutterstock

Printed in the United States of America

*McFarland & Company, Inc., Publishers
Box 611, Jefferson, North Carolina 28640
www.mcfarlandpub.com*

*For those men,
women and children
who were and still are
casualties of war*

"War is a racket. It always has been. It is possibly the oldest, easily the most profitable, surely the most vicious. It is the only one international in scope. It is the only one in which the profits are reckoned in dollars and the losses in lives."
—Smedley Butler, USMC

"Madness is precisely at the point of contact between the oneiric and the erroneous ... but while error is merely non-truth, while the dream neither affirms nor judges, madness fills the void of error with images...."
—Michel Foucault, *Madness and Civilization: A History of Insanity in the Age of Reason*

"I know now that a still, silent war has ravaged this country of my memories also; I know now it would be useless for me to look farther. Time lies between like a great gulf; I cannot get back."
—Erich Maria Remarque, *The Road Back*

Table of Contents

Acknowledgments   xi
Introduction   1

Part I. Marking Time
1. Dancing in the Dark   6
2. Like a Rolling Stone   14
3. What About Me   17
4. Miles from Nowhere   20
5. One Fine Day   21
6. Will the Circle Be Unbroken?   24
7. Keep On Pushing   29
8. Here, There and Everywhere   31
9. New Beginnings   35

Part II. Going South
10. Standing in the Shadows of Love   38
11. Sunny   40
12. Chain of Fools   42
13. Where Do We Go from Here?   44
14. Have You Ever Seen the Rain?   47
15. Darkness, Darkness   51
16. Who'll Stop the Rain?   53
17. Carry That Weight   57
18. Slippin' into Darkness   60

Table of Contents

Part III. Nothing for Nothing

19. Four Days Gone	64
20. Running on Empty	74
21. When You Awake	78
22. New Beginnings	80

Part IV. In the Zone

23. I Walk the Line	82
24. I Got Dreams to Remember	86
25. If You Want Me to Stay	89
26. There's a Hole in the Future	92
27. Goin' Out of My Head	94
28. Song of the Wind	96
29. Catch the Wind	102
30. My Back Pages	104
31. Ain't Nothing Like the Real Thing	107
32. New Beginnings	109

Part V. Waking Up

33. Slippin' into Darkness	112
34. Working Class Hero	116
35. Going Down Slowly	118
36. Be True to Your School	121
37. Homeward Bound	123
38. Where Did You Sleep Last Night?	124
39. Sweet Melissa	125
40. The Other Side of the Sky	129

Part VI. Back Stories

41. Going in Circles	134
42. A House Is Not a Home	140
43. Estate	144
44. Dedicated to You	148

Table of Contents

45. Sometimes I Feel Like a Motherless Child	151
46. Hurt	155

Part VII. Falling Forward

47. In a Sentimental Mood	160
48. Winter in America	171
49. (Who Wrote) The Book of Love?	186
50. Pavane	188
51. Rivers of My Fathers	191
52. When I'm Gone	197
Epilogue: Collateral Damage	199
Music/Playlist Credits	228
Books: A Short List	230
Index	233

Acknowledgments

An excerpt on dancing in Vietnam as *Solo by Gerald McCarthy* was initially published in *We Gotta Get Out of This Place—The Soundtrack of the Vietnam War* (p. 52–56). University of Massachusetts Press, 2015.* Reprinted with permission.

Excerpts originally titled *Coming Down, What I Did or Did Not Do* and *A Circle Round My Father* in earlier versions were first published in *The Deadly Writers Patrol*. University of Wisconsin, Madison, 2018. Reprinted with permission.

"Their Names Are Everywhere…" an essay on the dedication of the Vietnam Veterans Memorial in Washington, D.C., was originally published in an earlier version in *The National Catholic Reporter*, November 1982. Reprinted by permission of NCR Publishing Company, www.NCROnline.org.

Cliff Jumping was published in "A Force Outside Myself: Citizens Over 60 Speak," *McSweeney's Internet Tendency*, June 2, 2020. Reprinted with permission.

Four Days Gone appeared in *Consequence Forum*, Issue 14.1, Spring 2022. Reprinted with permission.

This is a work of nonfiction. On the advice of the editor, in most cases—except for the missing or the dead—the names of real persons have been changed. I have also jumbled the dates to some degree—call that my failing memory or a deliberate attempt to alter the timeline and to disremember the complete event.

---

* The introduction to *We Gotta Get Out of This Place*, written by Doug Bradley and Craig Lerner, is an excellent way to understand why music is so essential to the experiences of soldiers who served in Vietnam.

Acknowledgments

~ ~ ~

I owe many people my sincere thanks for help and encouragement, beginning with Dave and Sylvia Kelly who helped me through the most difficult times, giving me wise counsel and advice and love; the writers Judith Kitchen and Abraham Rothberg who both suggested I write this memoir before I knew how to begin; the author and cultural critic Mark Dery whose wit and keen insight were essential; the author Margot Mifflin who offered suggestions and honest support at key intervals; Bill Ehrhart for his help in getting the memoir to a senior editor; and Bruce Beyer, war resister (The Buffalo Nine) who refused to give up.

Special thanks to Sean Wilson, graphic designer at Aldan Press in Bardonia, New York, who helped with printing numerous hard copies of the manuscript and with restoring/enhancing the photographs.

~ ~ ~

And most of all my wife Michele who always, always listened to my stories with patience and kindness and whose love and help have kept me alive.

Introduction

My story begins in Vietnam—where I deplaned in 1966 as a naïve 18-year-old with no knowledge of the country, its culture, its people or their traditions. I survived physically, yet the invisible scars of the war have never left. I have learned how to live with post-traumatic stress disorder (PTSD)—and many people have helped me, sometimes without knowing it: my wife and sons, a few friends, and a therapist at the James A. Peters Veterans Hospital in the Bronx.

In the early summer of 1967, I was sent to Danang City to scrounge wooden pallets and other essential supplies for our 1st Engineer Battalion. The flame trees were in bloom, it was their season, and I was a short timer. I had less than a month left in country. Behind it all lived the shadows of what had happened to me, to all of us together and apart, alone and forever torn by dread and loss and lies. No one understands it, and no one should. It's not possible to understand.

Instead, there are catch phrases like *thank you for your service.* When what they really are saying is nothing at all ... they don't see you at all. They can't. If they did, there would be a tumult, a reckoning, something so strong and real everyone would hear it. Like a chorus of voices chanting, a cacophony of bells ringing over and over. And it would be deafening. Too many voices all calling at once. Now it's just too late. The line has gone dead. It's over. *Now there's just the dull ring tone, and no operator—just the automatic voice repeating over and over. Sorry. The number you have dialed is no longer in service.*

Less than a month later, I had to hitchhike to the Danang

Introduction

airfield because there were no PCs (personnel carriers) available that morning in July. When I finally came back from Vietnam after my 13-month tour, it seemed as if the flames had followed me; the whole country was on fire—race riots in Newark, New York, Detroit, Buffalo, Minneapolis, Atlanta and many more cities. I knew then I would carry the war with me forever.

"Memory is our root system," the poet William Matthews wrote, and for me music is a trigger for memory—a connection to both the past and present. Each section of this narrative is a song title—a song to evoke the episode, serve as an ironic counterpoint, or capture an emotional connection to the event(s).*

There are many ways to read this book. My original concept was random—free association—*skip around*. For me, the narrative is a long series of memories—all connected, some occurring and reoccurring at random intervals, and often memories I have no control over—so they recur at odd moments (for example, at an interview with the provost at my former college, who asked me when I would retire; in a waiting room of a doctor's office; while shopping for groceries at a supermarket; or even at a café in another country) when someone passes by and triggers the flashback to another time.

I like Julio Cortázar's idea (from *Hopscotch*) to read it back to front, or you can follow my own original schematic (1, 19, 41, 2, 11, 23, 13, 33, 14, 21, 26, 17, then your choice) or read it *as usual* from beginning to end.

Certain repetitive passages are deliberate because repeating a memory mimics my own issues with the past—for me a natural thing, and I hope repetition adds some cohesiveness. To quote another writer: "Many were afflicted with a strange mania which caused them to repeat the same word, or continually to make the same gesture when they chanced to raise their heads and look at one another, they were choked with sobbing at the sight of the fearful ravages shown on the faces of their fellows. Some had ceased to

---

* *Moving Again, Rising and Falling* (Boston, Massachusetts: Little, Brown & Co., 1979).

Introduction

suffer, and to while away the hours, told stories of the dangers they had escaped" (Flaubert, *Salammbô*).*

The sections in *italics* are a deliberate way to set off a difficult or disturbing experience, even a traumatic memory that does not go away; in fact, this is my attempt to describe how even when one is not ready for it that an invasive memory comes back, interrupting the narration. Call it one way to explain the effects of PTSD—how the person who is *under the hammer* of it, has no control over when or where it will appear, like a shadow that comes into a sunlit room and suddenly alters the feel of the room.

~ ~ ~

---

* Gustave Flaubert, *Salammbô*, trans. E. Powys Mather (New York: Berkley Publishing, 1955).

Part I
Marking Time

1

Dancing in the Dark

Race and class were always central issues in my war. I was too ignorant then to understand how much of a role they played in our purpose for being there, in the ways we waged the war, and in the young men who had been trained to fight it. I was 18 when I went overseas, and a few months past my 19th birthday when I returned. I didn't think about consequences or about reasons. I was all for a life of sensation, and I made my decisions based on impulse and poor judgment. Now, looking back, I like to believe I may have learned a few things about what happened to me and to the men I knew in that war. And central to our days there and always in the background was the soul music we listened to when we could.

After the crackers burned a wooden cross in front of Doc Brown's tent and our outfit had packed up and moved north by ship to join Alpha Company near an old French parapet along Highway One, and after the war came closer with nightly mortar and rocket attacks; but before *new guys* started coming over in groups of twos and threes; and before the battalion armorer got sent to Cambodia to deliver the new M-16s to the company that was not really there; and before the gunnery sergeant told five of us to hide from the inspector general during the battalion inspection because we looked too dirty; and after TK got NSU—short for non-specific urethritis—which he claimed he got from drinking bad beer in the village, but others believed he got from having sex with one of the Coca-Cola girls near the base; and before Puff and I borrowed a dump truck and brought back 50 stolen cases of POM juice and an electric typewriter for the gunnery sergeant; and before the sweet smell of Park Lane Boulevard and deep smoke penetrated the compound; and after the captain

1. Dancing in the Dark

flipped out and tried to bust me for talking with the Vietnamese by the RR tracks, and Gramps thought he saw ghosts of water buffalo on the road, and Jack the Jip dumped garbage on the children in the dump; but before Martin went AWOL on a garbage run to Danang; and after Shaley came rolling out of the night on a TD-15 forklift drinking cans of San Miguel beer; and before Max and Stanton and JT went missing on Operation Union II; and after Morro became the general's driver; and after the winter rains; we used to dance with each other at the enlisted man's club on muggy, late nights. *I know ... dancing in a combat zone, but that's what it was—and it happened.*

The cross burning was one outcome of the dancing. Imagine those good old boys sitting in the back of the enlisted man's club—a tin-roofed shack the 3rd Engineers had left for us when they moved north to the DMZ. Imagine what they thought when they saw white guys dancing with Black guys to the soul music on the makeshift jukebox in the club. It was the dancing that popped open the tab on the canned hatred that had been welling up just below the surface of our days and nights. "That's all it took ... just one look."*

We had a song about the road—modeled on the Drifters hit "On Broadway." Our version was "On Highway One." The dancing began after dark. I learned how to dance there at night. I learned line dancing and break dancing and solo dancing. I learned how to lean into the music and get my hips and shoulders moving with the beat. I learned a lot from the young men who taught me how to dance—Ward and Gramps, Louis and Turner. I learned about being Black in the Jim Crow south, and about double standards in Ward's Chicago. I learned to listen to others and to see and feel the racism in even the simplest things: job assignments, guard duty, and patrols. I developed a kinship and community with my Black comrades, and I learned a respect for them as individuals and as men. This kinship arose out of my rejection of the *good ole boy, line 'em up at the bar* crap the Marines were always running down. I trusted the brothers I knew, and I liked them because they too rejected the macho nonsense and the pseudo-tough guy crap. And I knew they had

---

* From song "Just One Look" by Doris Troy.

Part I—Marking Time

my back. I knew they would always stand up to whatever we had to face.

I grew to love the music we listened to and danced to on those nights after the spring rains came, and I grew to love those "brothers," too. For me, this *soul music* has always served as an enduring wellspring of memory and inspiration. Whenever or wherever I have been, whatever bad times or hard situations I have faced, whatever moments of joy I may have had—the *soul music* from those days still has emotional power and depth. Call it nostalgia if you like, but it's far from that—it is more realism and a reality check for me. It reminds me of where I have been, that the combat engineer battalion I served in overseas was over 40 percent Black and Latino, that the things I witnessed there and afterwards coming home would not tuck into "file and forget."*

~ ~ ~

First, we'd drink all the PBRs or Buds or whatever cans of beer they had cold, and when they had to start icing some more that's when the dancing would start. In our outfit, there was never that much beer anyhow—and some nights they just ran out. The soul brothers were the ones who got it started—Ward, Gramps, Louis and Turner and one or two of the other men. They began to dance and pushed us—three or four reluctant white guys—into dancing too. Before long, we would be dancing together to the music from the jukebox in the corner. We'd dance with each other under the tin roof of the club in the early dark. Doc Brown and Big Mike and a few others would be playing Whist and the rest of us would be dancing. It was always soul music that we danced to, and it wasn't as though you had a partner or anything, but we did dance with each other. The brothers would help us white dudes so we'd get our shoulders and upper bodies into it, and we'd forget where we were, what was going on, and for a song or two it seemed as if we were somewhere else, living a double life in the world and pretending we were cooler than we really were, dapping and throwing down hands and learning about

---

* From a poem by Horace Coleman.

1. Dancing in the Dark

the *soul* of it. One time even the gunnery sergeant in charge of the HQ office joined in. It was a gift our Black friends gave us—for me, it was a gift of understanding and an awakening to a world I had never known much about. It was a gift of music and a love for music that still evokes the feeling of youth and earnestness and possibility.

~ ~ ~

The best songs were the ones we knew already; the songs that had been playing on tape decks and radios in advanced training and in Pendleton and then later in the gut bars of Okinawa and finally in the first few nights in country at the airbase in Saigon. Songs like the Temptations' "Don't Look Back." "If it's love that you're running from, there's no hiding place/you can't run/you can't hide." Most of us "white boys" were 18 or 19, and although it may sound strange or unrealistic after all this time—we were uninhibited by race or sex—at least for the short time on those nights when we could forget the things that divided us, those things that would later come between us. Maybe we were ignorant then—especially the youngest of us. I suppose it seemed weird to those old-timers who hung in the corners and gave us dirty looks, the ones who nursed their beers and sat back smugly, smoking. But we didn't care. It was as if we were in the moment, and the moment was about the music and the dancing, and how quickly time had passed, how much had happened to us already.

Maybe we were free because we didn't know where we were going—there was a fresh feeling and an openness about us that had not been sullied by the war yet and had not been changed by experience and hatred. My friend Ward would say we were naïve, and I suppose we were naïve about the things that were happening back in the world, about the things that had already happened when we were still in high school. And if you don't believe naïveté, then let's say that perhaps some of the men I knew then deliberately tried to turn their backs to the truths they knew about from growing up, if only to escape them for a little while. You had to get away from your own past—step out of the history you were aware of that had shaped you and channeled you into the war in the first place. Most of us were

Part I—Marking Time

still volunteers then—the draftees had not started to come overseas yet. And we did learn; it just took longer.

Maybe the songs themselves spoke to what we felt we'd left behind; maybe they spoke to our need to be ignorant of what we should have known. Songs like "Since I Lost My Baby." "The sun is shining, there's plenty of light…." These songs were about love, about the "world" we'd left that was not there anymore; maybe it had never been there except in our imaginations. Songs like "The Tracks of My Tears" or "The Same Old Song" or the song some brothers sang a cappella in basic training—"What Love Has Joined Together." These songs fed our dreams and were good dancing tunes. I think we danced with each other because we were in love with those dreams—with the lies we had lived with while growing up, with the fantasies that had fueled our patriotism, our earnestness and our belief that we could change things, that we could make a difference. The soul music we danced to then was filled with a kind of nostalgia for a time that did not exist any longer, but we could not know this—it was impossible for us to know how the war would change us and shape our lives and the future we thought was ours. The sad thing about innocence is that it has a kind of effervescence, a notion that all things are possible, a feeling that surges above what is true.

~ ~ ~

Another group of songs had a double edge—songs like "Jimmy Mack" or "Shake Me, Wake Me." They cut both ways: you could feel the truth in them, the truth about leaving home and perhaps not coming back, and you could see another reality there too, as if the war was a dream and one day we would wake up. And that waking would have its own terrible consequences. Songs like "On Broadway" that we turned into "On Highway One"—by making up our own lyrics to hit the irony of our real estrangement from "the world" and from any kind of love, even if it were love fed on youth and fantasy. And there were songs—like "Keep On Pushing" that spoke to a world we would inherit, but they were positive—suggesting we might overcome the differences of race and class. Finally, there was James Brown, whose song "Papa's Got a Brand New Bag" ushered in a new

1. Dancing in the Dark

era of music and a new wave of songs that would get at the heart of the times; it was a song with a subtle subtext: *watch out, beware, get ready.*

~ ~ ~

Now I know the cross burning was just the beginning; this act would bring us into a new phase, a different reality, and now I no longer believe what I believed then in that Year of the Goat near the South China Sea. Maybe it was because most of us had only been six months in country, or maybe because the bad stuff hadn't happened yet, the hard deaths and crazy episodes that waited right out of reach beyond the villages below. And the Tet Offensive was still eight months away—and Martin Luther King's assassination almost eleven months away. Or maybe as my friend Ward from Chicago warned me, *"You don't get what's happening here, Mac, you don't see how we're divided and how we can't come back from those divisions without a lot of stuff changing."* That night we were listening to the album *Sketches of Spain* by Miles Davis on Armed Forces Radio in Ward's cube in the Comm platoon tent, and the first rains had just started to fall.

"You don't know man, because you don't get what it is to be Black—you can't feel it. Remember that night the wise-ass dude Stanton tried to intimidate you and Gonzalez? Remember? What the hell could you do? That's what those guys are about," Ward said, *"intimidation. And it will get worse, you watch, man."* Ward was right. He knew we were all daydreaming, drifting off with the music and with our own kinship to the songs we danced to in the club on those spring nights. And it did get worse—two nights later JP shot all the lights out in his tent. He wanted to sleep, he said. He'd been out on a sweep and was tired. Things started to get crazy right after that.

~ ~ ~

It is easier to see our ignorance for what it was, an ignorance spawned by our youthful disregard for authority and reality, a way we all had of not seeing what we should have recognized. Many years later the poet Sonia Sanchez would tell my writing class at Attica prison: "If you are here on purpose, it means you'll come back on

Part I—Marking Time

purpose."* And I know she was speaking about prison and recidivism, and the racism inherent in the penal system and society, but instead I remembered the men—especially the *soul brothers* I had served with in Vietnam who did come back to face the same things again and again at home. We came back to different Americas, yet because of them I would never see my home the same way again.

There's a photograph of Ward, Louis and Turner from my last month in country, and I still carry it in my wallet—its edges torn, the color faded. It reminds me of one of my last nights with them and some of the other men, sitting in the gunnery sergeant's office, smoking cigarettes and talking.

Suddenly, Martinez blurted out, "Mac, don't go back there and forget about us, don't let it slip away." There was a sudden hush after he'd said it—Martinez was new to the outfit—but we liked him for his attitude.

Today, what still binds me to the men I knew there is this sense of loss and displacement. It's easy to be critical when you have the force of history behind you, when you see the deaths we witnessed in Vietnam and afterwards were connected, and I confess that the *soul music* we loved and danced to *was* an escape—a return to a world we thought we knew but did not know, a glimpse into a time that was an essential part of us. In this way, music was our youth and a connection to the things we shared: class and work and war; it was essential because it did not divide us or stress our differences.

The Same Old Song
by Gerald McCarthy

> The night the crackers burned a cross
> in front of Doc Brown's tent,
>
> Turner and I pulled the late guard,
> watched as the smoke rose over the company yard,
>
> and I could sense his anger
> across the close dark of our sandbagged hole,
>
> when he sighed—I knew
> they'd get around to this.

---

* Sonia Sanchez, Attica Correctional Facility, Attica, New York (6/14/1978).

1. Dancing in the Dark

Staring through the starlight scope,
I thought I saw that burning cross
   spread its flames beyond
the headlands, reddening the sky—

until dawn took me by surprise,
raw daylight settling around us like a wound.

~ ~ ~

2

Like a Rolling Stone

I failed at a lot of things, and I didn't learn. It started with failing as a son. I remember the way my father looked at me the afternoon he drove me to the bus station after I had enlisted in the Marines; his face a mix of sadness and resignation, set with his stubborn avowal to let me have my own way. My friends had stood by outside our home on the evening my father signed me in—I was 17—the recruiter gave him all three copies and before he signed each one, he'd look up at me and asked: *"Are you sure you want to do this?"*

Worried, grim, my father's hands gripped the steering wheel of the humpback, black 1950 Dodge. My stepmother sat in the wide back seat, believing it "would make a man of me." *A man*, I thought, sitting in the front seat for the first time as Bob Dylan sang "Like a Rolling Stone" on the car radio, and I turned it up to remember the words, to blot out my stepmother's questions, my father's silence.

And the downtown passed, the houses along the river pushed up against each other in a sleepy wash of sunlight, the red-brick factory buildings with their windows broken, boarded up, letting out the workers for the midday break. We passed the junkyard near the mouth of the creek, and I thought of the weekday smells of the tanneries belching the acrid, pungent, leathery odors; the Friday night sweat smells and cooking smells; sauce bubbling on kitchen stoves; the windows steamy from the hot water for pasta; the sausage smells of delis and pizza joints; and the deeper, sadder odors of spilled beer and tiredness and sleep. I could see the terraced hills, the gardens drooping with tomatoes, homegrown grapes, the squash spreading its yellow flowers. And I remembered the hot afternoons giving way to the smells of wine and cigar smoke. A bus ride from a factory town

2. Like a Rolling Stone

to the state capitol and then *the hook*. I don't remember what my father said as they left me off, my stepmother looking away toward the new mall site. I know I looked back to watch the car recede—its fat, black blur with two figures up in front caught in the early afternoon traffic.

Waiting in the bus station—I remembered how I'd run away in the late spring—for the second time. My parents had decided to take my brother and me for a weekend stay in the Finger Lakes at a motel in Canandaigua. I wanted no part of it, and when they were distracted with the checkin at the motel, I got out of the car and started to hitchhike in the other direction—the way we had come. A car pulled over and picked me up right away. The driver said he was going as far as Cortland—which was out of the way but would get me closer to home. I knew my parents would be crazy by now—me spoiling their plans for a weekend—but I wanted no part of the trip. I was 17 and almost out of high school, and I knew I had to change things, I had to act to get away from them and from the way they had control over me and everything I did.

After it started to get late—I'd been trying to hitch a ride out of Cortland for over two hours—I worried I wouldn't make it before dark. Then at last a kind, older man picked me up. He said he was going all the way to Endicott, and I knew I could walk home from there.

By 9 o'clock that night I was walking down Main Street to our house, and I realized my parents had beaten me home. I knew how angry they'd be, so I just sat outside on the patio and waited for them to notice me. When they did, my father came outside and asked how I had gotten home. *Hitchhiking* was all I said. My parents knew something had changed for good.

Less than a week later, I went to the recruiting office in Binghamton and told the recruiter there I wanted to enlist. He told me I had to get my father to sign me in since I was underage. He promised me I'd be standing five inches taller after boot camp—and "Don't forget you get the dress blue uniform." I knew this was a come on—only **one man** got dress blues out of boot camp—the guy who scored the highest in every category and made PFC upon graduation. And that was the deal.

Part I—Marking Time

Now in the bus station waiting room, I wondered about what I'd done. Too late to turn back. Too late. And I remembered my high school student teacher Leslee, who had tried to tell me not to go. But I had already enlisted.

~ ~ ~

3

What About Me

After we left Binghamton, a young guy got on the Greyhound at a rural stop, and the first thing he said to me was that he'd enlisted in the Marines after the Army had turned him down. He was a farm boy from the country around Greene, New York, and I liked him right off for his plainness and honesty. He was tall and stoop-shouldered and had terrible acne and thick-rimmed glasses that made him look 20 or more instead of 17. His name was Gary Shaley.

Seeing my ditty bag, the look, that leanness, lisping—*"You're goin' to Albany"*—more of a statement than a question, he moved into the seat next to me. I didn't feel like talking but he pressed it, trying to smooth away his own tears, his own way of leaving. And then the bus rolling up and down almost like a drunk weaving through a crowded space, like the deck of a ship, you know, contagious—like someone stumbling makes others stumble. The way we both looked out the window toward the names of places passing by until we knew we would not return to that day in July when we rode to the enlistment center together.

We shared the ride to Albany, then dinner that night in a cafeteria downtown where they took the government coupons and the double room they gave us in a government pay-by-coupons hotel. We were sworn in together, we flew down to boot camp together, and we spent 13 weeks in basic training and then advanced training. Yet, after that, I never saw Gary again until the late winter of 1967.

It was the night our battalion moved into Danang. We'd disembarked off ships in the afternoon, and I'd been assigned to ride guard on the TD-15 forklifts that were carrying boxes of gear from the harbor area to battalion headquarters. We had moved the outfit from

Part I—Marking Time

Chu Lai to Danang in less than three days. Now we had to unload the cargo and gear. It was a thirty-minute trip through the outskirts of the Danang airbase and the small villages that surrounded it. The night was dark and cool for February.

When I saw him, he came out of the dusk almost ghostlike—driving the TD-15 forklift, half standing, half sitting atop the platform of the lift in the open air. At first, he didn't recognize me but shouted down for me to climb up. I'd done two trips already and was waiting for the new driver to come when I looked up and saw him.

Shaley—sunburned, older, still wearing those thick military lenses—but now the flip-up shades. The twilight came on so fiercely as we rode back to the new compound—through the villages, boondocking it—drinking warm beer up there on the driver's seat. He'd been in country three months already, and like me, they'd changed his specialty—he had been designated as underwater demolitions and now he was a forklift driver. We shot the beers he had with him and tilted back, and then too soon his ride with me was over and another driver took his place. And as I watched him go I thought about boot camp again, how his parents had come down for graduation, and how they took him on a picnic afterward, inviting me along too, a second son for the day.

That night in Danang we rode through those villages together, oblivious to the danger on the open highway, telling each other about where we'd been, how we got there, Shaley winging off like some gangly scarecrow—that crazy country boy screech he had, and the sadder look he covered up—like some young Ichabod making his base-camp trip alone. A year later when I was locked up in the Brooklyn Brig, I got a forwarded postcard from him. Gary said that he was okay, home and safe. There was no return address.

On the Wall

His name was Brent I. Griggs and the guys who knew him from basic training in San Diego called him Ike. I met him for the first time in Camp Pendleton where they sent all of us to get special

3. What About Me

training before going overseas. On our 20-mile forced march with full packs and rifles, Griggs said to me that we had to help Gutierrez carry his gear.

"*He ain't gonna be able to hump it with all this stuff—he only weighs 95 pounds himself.*" And Griggs took the majority of gear in Gutierrez's pack and put it in with his own, and I took Gutierrez's rifle. And that's how it started.

When we got through with training, they shipped us all overseas—first to Okinawa to get our shots and stow our winter uniforms, and then after three days we went *south* to Vietnam. There's a photo of us standing around at Camp Hansen in Okinawa. We look pale and starched and young in our stateside utilities. Griggs was older than most of us—22. Gutierrez, Proctor, Angelo and I were 18. The night before we left, we all got crazy drunk in the bars, and I remember Griggs sitting on a bar stool after he'd spent all his money. For me, Griggs was like all the rest of us—we never had a chance. There was no break-in period; there was no recovery from the flights and the shots and the side effects of all the shots they'd hit us with. No wonder now realizing how many boys died on entry—a patrol on their second day in country—and no way to get ready for it. Too young. I was six months into 18. Most of the others were the same. I would have been better on a second tour—I could take the heat and could live with it; I knew how to deal.

~ ~ ~

4.

Miles from Nowhere

The last stop before basic training had been a bus station in a small town in South Carolina. It was in the early hours of the morning and we'd been traveling all day and all night—a busload of new recruits with half an hour to spend before we started up again.

Some guys played the jukebox, drinking tall orange sodas and slouching on the wooden benches. The window for the package counter was shut, the dull iron bars damp with the cool night air, its eye closed up against the night. I remember one boy who pushed a postcard into the mail slot, "A last note home," he said to me as I looked at him. We'd been sworn in together that morning in Albany.

Outside, the oozing sickly smell of swamplands and paper mills seemed to be growing closer, choking us, waking us from the 3 a.m. doze of travel—as if childhood were ending there; someone playing "Homeward Bound" by Simon & Garfunkel, as if it too were a sad laugh at us.

It seemed as if all we had been before was caught like the moths on the screens of that waystation shack, like the wisp of a curtain lifted away from the checked paint; a penetrating odor of sulfur mixed with magnolia; a smell that would follow us like the music would as the bus stood there, idling—a signal of the months, the years ahead.

~ ~ ~

5

One Fine Day

Wake-up Call

We got to Parris Island at 4 a.m. Through the open windows of the Trailways bus, I could smell the acrid smoke from paper mills and the deeper odor of swamp gas and tiredness. Or was it that we were tired? We'd been traveling all day—most of us from different parts of the East Coast: New York, Pennsylvania, Delaware, Washington, D.C., Virginia, even North Carolina. And in the dim light of early morning some of us were dozing, nodding off—until the bus stopped and a sergeant seemed to jump up into the aisle, yelling—*"All right, assholes, get off the damn bus! And move it now, ladies! Move it! Let's go, let's go, let's go! Wake the fuck up!"*

After the bus emptied out, the drill instructors started shouting, *"Line up, you silly ass fucks, line up your dumb asses ... you ain't no civilian turds anymore, you're fucking recruit turds now, stupid ass recruit motherfuckers, dumber than shit."* And after we tried to stand in a line with our overnight bags, someone laughed—a tall, lanky guy we'd picked up someplace south of Charlotte. The sergeant who had climbed aboard the bus walked over to him and stuck his face right up close to the guy's face—*"What the fuck you laughing at, you stupid shit? Huh?"* Then he pulled the kid out of line and dragged him toward the wooden building.

"You gonna be the last one in now, you country-ass fuck."

In Albany, our group from upstate New York had been sworn in together at the Marine Corps Office—we had physicals and papers to sign, and they gave us coupons to have lunch downtown before they drove us to the airport. It was the first time most of us had ever been on an airplane—the "slow hawk" as someone called it—Mohawk

Part I—Marking Time

Airlines—a bumpy ride to somewhere in North Carolina and then a long bus ride to the Marine recruit depot at Parris Island. And that's how it began. First thing they did was to intimidate us—all 75 of us in turn—one by one or in groups.

Now the intake comes back out of chronological order and in pieces—the haircuts first, three drill instructors yelling out orders—seeming to be in all places at once, sowing a kind of confusion and fear, shouting at each one of us. Then the clothing issue, the new utilities, the cap—the white T-shirt; tagging and marking our civilian clothing and the stuff we'd brought with us ... to be sent back home. By the time we were tagged and given our serial numbers, by the time we had our photos taken—shaved heads shining back at us and new military eyeglasses for me as well—by the time we saw ourselves as we were, it felt as if we'd come from another planet, as if we belonged to a new race, a new breed of people. And that's what they wanted, you see—catching us off guard, sowing a sense of mistrust and fear, of what would happen next. By 8 o'clock in the morning when the sun was starting to hit those wooden buildings and you could feel the heat—it seemed as if we'd been up for days—and then in a shrill whine of siren there was a call to line up for breakfast, a 15-minute gasp before going back to get measured and fitted and pick up our "chrome dome" helmets.

At noon, riding the "cattle car" to our barracks, a young, red-haired kid with freckles started to talk to the guy next to him and the D.I. on the car leaned over and, with a flick of his large index finger, snapped the kid's lip and broke the skin, the blood streaming down onto the boy's new T-shirt, tears welling up in his eyes as the sergeant said, *"Shut the fuck up, asshole."*

At the barracks—what the sergeant called "Disneyland" because they were newer than the other battalion barracks, made out of brick and concrete instead of wood—things got crazy really fast. Upstairs, on the third floor—our home for the next few months—the head sergeant in charge of the platoon stood up on a footlocker as he started to call off our names and assign us to our beds.

"Goddamit, Sergeant Taylor, what the fuck have we got here—what a sorry ass bunch of dumbass lookin' turds—what have you

5. *One Fine Day*

brought me, huh? I mean what the fuck is this?" Sgt. Taylor, the man who had popped the kid's lip, just looked down the long deck and shouted, *"Get down and give me some push-ups, ladies, fifty push-ups right fucking now. "*

And as we began, dropping our seabags and gear, another sergeant came up and started to yell at a guy who was having some issues with the push-ups. *"What the fuck is wrong with you, asshole? Huh? What's the fucking problem here?"* And he dragged the boy up to his feet and punched him hard in the gut.

"Get with the fucking program, turd."

The kid was one of the guys from upstate New York who had left with us that day.

"You look like you need to lose some weight, fat boy. You like eating cheeseburgers, turd?"

And the kid, who was six feet tall and big, shrugged. The sergeant punched him hard again and the kid barfed.

"Sheet!" he screamed. *"Now look what you've gone and done, you sorry ass motherfucker. You better go get something to clean that up, asshole."* And he dragged the boy down the length of the barracks to the mop closet and made him get a bucket of water and a mop. His name was Jim Galutz. He made PFC in basic training, he was wounded in April 1967 and he later died of those wounds in Bethesda, Maryland.

~ ~ ~

6

Will the Circle Be Unbroken?

In boot camp when we got to the rifle range, if you didn't get a good score for the day, meaning you went UNC—there were about 15 of us who were in that boat—instead of dinner that night, you got to have a circle with one of the drill instructors.

He sat behind you in a chair and you sat on the floor with your eyes open. Then you were required to recite the definition of *trigger squeeze*: "a slow, steady pressure to the rear until the sear is engaged and the trigger is released, sir."

During your recital, the D.I.—Sgt. Taylor—would slap you hard across the side of your neck. The assembled crew in semi-circle would tell the drill instructor if you blinked, and if you did, you had to recite the definition again and again until you did it without blinking. The D.I. was a big guy and hit you with a slap that left a good mark on the side of your neck. It took over an hour for us to get through all 15 guys, and of course many of us blinked more than once. That night we had an orange for dinner.

I guess we must have gotten the message, since we all qualified. As it turned out, my problem was an inability to close one eye, my left, while keeping my right eye open. (Now I know this is called lazy eye.) The next day at the range the D.I., Sgt. Taylor, got down with me when I was firing and realized I had to learn to shoot with both eyes open or block my left eye. He swore and said, "Shit, you fucking turd, you got no control over that left eye." To compensate, he tucked my ID in front of the left eye—and I qualified. I never had a problem with jerking the trigger; I just couldn't shut the left eye. Later he said, "You gotta learn how to shoot with both eyes open, ain't no big deal, private."

6. Will the Circle Be Unbroken?

It was too late to make up the two days prior to learning this, so I only qualified as a marksman, the lowest ranking.

~ ~ ~

Boot Camp Blues

The Cake

My Aunt Flo and Aunt Eleanor sent me a cake and some cookies they'd baked for me while I was still in boot camp sometime during September, and when I heard the head drill instructor call my name during mail call, I knew something was up.

"What's this package from New York, Private turd?" he asked.

"Sir. The private does not know, sir."

"Well, you better open this god damn box right now, private." When I did, I saw the homemade cookies and a large cake as well.

The senior D.I. kind of laughed. "Well, what the hell is this, private, huh?

Looks like some kind of present, private. Is it your birthday?"

"No, sir," I said.

"Well, you can't be eating this kinda thing in my house, private. You better just give it to Sgt. Marto here as a little present. That ok with you, sergeant?"

They both shook their heads and Sgt. Matthews looked over at me and said, "Now you get down on my deck and give me 50 push-ups, private cake-and-cookie-man. Get to it!"

Private McDoo and Private Duke Get Special Treatment

Private McDoo had the top bunk above me. Every night before we went to sleep, we all had to stand at attention in front of our racks (beds) in our white skivvies and T-shirts with our washed tan belt around our neck. McDoo always forgot to wash his belt or at least get it wet in the shower so it would appear he had washed it.

Part I—Marking Time

Some nights the youngest D.I. was on—call him Sgt. Marto—who enjoyed any kind of sadistic punishment and who also had never been overseas. When he was on duty, he would strangle McDoo with his own belt when he saw that McDoo had not washed it. Now the private who stood directly across from me on the "starboard" side of the barracks, he would crack a smile and get me to smile too. And so as McDoo got strangled, I got punched in the gut and had to do 50 push-ups.

~ ~ ~

Private Duke was a Canadian volunteer who came down to basic training with long hair, and who immediately got himself on the wrong side of every drill instructor. They all hated him because they thought he was a hippie. He was from somewhere in the Canadian countryside, barely five feet tall and very thin, and they enjoyed tormenting him. One night, they hung him up on an overhead steel pipe with his armpits on the pipe, then they took his belt and pulled it over his suspended arms—Sgt. Marto took special pleasure in punching Private Duke in the stomach and watching him swing back and forth. This went on for at least 30 minutes until the senior drill instructor called it off.

~ ~ ~

Dirty Work

Yes. You got it, there were nasty little blanket parties for certain guys, too. One night Sgt. Marto directed some of the others to give Private Lenny L. a blanket party—throw a blanket over him in his bunk after lights out and pummel him for 10 minutes, so he got the message to get with the four-mile run we had to do every day.

Lenny was overweight and the drill instructors were always on him to keep up and move on. They told him he was bound for STB or Special Training Battalion if he didn't make the grade. STB was pure hell—PT all day long, breaking big rocks into little ones, digging outside latrines. It went on until the private who got sent there was "physically fit" to be a Marine recruit. As it turned out, they did

6. *Will the Circle Be Unbroken?*

end up sending Lenny to STB, but before our final forced march into the dunes and sleep out in small tents Lenny got a release and came back to the platoon. He looked different—thinner ... more determined. And the reason I remember him is he was on the flight down to Parris Island with our group of upstate New York boys who were sworn in together in Albany.

Lenny was awarded the Bronze Star for his actions helping others in 1968—on his second tour in Vietnam.

~ ~ ~

Respect Yourself

A central aspect of Marine basic training was to call all recruits "ladies" or "girls" or to suggest any feeling for another person was a *feminine* trait. One of the running count cadence songs was "Jody's got your girl" and the drill instructor would call the cadence—how a guy comes along and takes your girlfriend. Or another classic was "I know a girl and her name is ------- if she won't do it her sister will. Left, right, left." And more choruses, each one more profane than the next.

If you messed up on a drill or an inspection or a detail, you were called a "pussy" or a "sissie" or the like.

In his fine memoir about the Marines in Korea, *The Last Parallel*, Martin Russ notes, "As a Marine, one almost feels obliged to conceal any emotion except anger. To show sympathy for instance, would suggest effeminacy" (p. 13).

And there it is. As the anti-feminine behavior is literally pounded into you, it is no wonder that some Marines develop a hatred for women and for those who "feel," especially for someone less macho or masculine. I came away from boot camp with a hardened attitude toward many things—and it took years for me to feel empathy in a "real" way, maybe to feel anything at all. Or to echo Russ: "The need to cache a feeling with a four-letter word and protect yourself from ridicule." One expression from Vietnam in 1967 was "give a shit"; so popular I had it engraved on my cigarette lighter.

Part I—Marking Time

~ ~ ~

Final Inspection Practice

During our practice for the final "inspection," which was really a real practice with a real captain who asked us questions, well, during the inspection it came my turn to give the specifications for the M-1 rifles we were using in boot camp. I rattled off the specs and was incorrect on the actual *weight* of the rifle. This would not have been such a bad thing, but our D.I., Sgt. Taylor, had told us that everyone should follow the lead of the private who answers the question. So, seven other dudes gave the same wrong answer that I gave, and after the "practice" was over, while knocking off the 100 push-ups for Sgt. Taylor, he kept on yelling at me, *"You dumb fucking turd—why didn't you just say you didn't know?"* Instead, the captain caught on to the deal and started to ask different questions of every private. We all learned something from that inspection.

Photograph of the author at boot camp, September 1965. The first time I heard the expression: "Eat the apple, fuck the Corps."

~ ~ ~

7

Keep On Pushing

Infantry Training Regiment (ITR)
Camp Lejeune, Fall 1965

Although the official records online tell a different story, we spent less than 11 weeks in boot camp and then were sent to Camp Lejeune, North Carolina, where we spent less than four weeks in the Infantry Training Regiment or ITR. None of the things we learned there were really essential to what was happening to our guys in Vietnam back then, but we learned how to fire bazookas and grenade launchers and how to toss hand grenades. We learned again how to crawl under barbed wire with machine guns firing at us, we learned what it was like to carry a forty-pound pack, and we learned to take care of one another.

They were still doing search-and-destroy patrols back then, so I am glad I didn't get sent to a line outfit when I finally went overseas. I knew I was still too young to get it, too young to understand what was really going on, too stupid to see the problems I faced. I tried hard. I did the forced marches, the practices with weapons, and it felt good to be free of the continuous craziness of boot camp. At least, we were now officially Marines; most of us were still privates, but there were a few PFCs who had made the rank in boot camp. I was still 17 and still had those Hollywood notions of heroes and glory. I was dumb. And looking back, this training didn't do anything to address the real war and the kind of things most units were up against in 1966 and 1967.

One positive take-away from ITR, as we called it, was the friendships we made—and even though most of us would never see one

Part I—Marking Time

other again or be assigned to the same outfits, there was a feeling of being in the same place together and a sharing a common *bond*—although now I think it was more a sense of how we were in this thing and we had to help each other.

Five or six of us were all going on a train to Washington after the training was complete at Camp Lejeune. I was headed for New York City as were one or two others—but we all had to go to Washington, D.C., which was the central hub for the railroad. That afternoon in the station terminal each of us had two big seabags with all our gear, and we were still wearing those bulky, brimmed service caps until a young lance corporal came up to our group, saw we were fresh out of training with our single National Defense Ribbons, and busted our chops by calling us all to attention and then laughing as he said, "Why don't you guys shift to the 'piss cutters'" as garrison caps were called back then, "and give yourselves a break?"

Most of us listened and stowed our bulky caps away and put on our "piss cutters." It did make it easier to lug those bags on and off the trains. Three of us headed north to New York, and the rest of the group went wherever their trains were going. It was November and getting cool in the east. I'd been away since July.

8

Here, There and Everywhere

I came home by train from boot camp and ITR toward the end of November. It was the old Erie-Lackawanna Line that ran upstate out of New Jersey to Scranton and through Northern Pennsylvania and into the Catskills to Binghamton and then Endicott and points north and west.

In those days they still called it the *Phoebe Snow*. I watched the countryside roll past, the leaves falling, those familiar names of the towns and lakes I knew as a boy. They still resonate today—Starrucca, Susquehanna, Deposit, Hales Eddy, Silver Lake, Quaker Lake, Island Lake. And I thought about all the adventures I'd had in those places, night fishing, hiking up to the overlook on "high rock" where six lakes were visible in the distance. I thought about the warm summer nights I'd spent with my neighbors who took me with them to their cottage on a lake, and how good it felt to fall asleep outside on their screened-in porch listening to the night sounds of the lake, the frogs in the shallows and the crickets out in the night woods. I forced myself to remember why I had left home in the first place—just to keep from drifting off into some romantic pipedream of my own past.

The conductor in my car helped me get those two seabags into the doorway. They must have weighed 40 pounds each. And I stumbled down off the narrow steel stairs onto the wooden platform. It was one of those bright fall days with both light and shadow, and a kind of warmth grew in the leaves and the sunlight. And this light seemed to grow around me, as if I had changed, as if I were older—when I was still only 17, one week short of my birthday. I felt older, stronger, sure of myself.

Part I—Marking Time

I made a phone call to my father from the pay telephone booth outside the old station. Then I sat down on the wooden bench and waited. I felt an odd nostalgia for the station, the platform, the sense of how different it seemed.

I remembered the fall days when my grandfather was still alive—those days when he would unload his freight car full of boxes of California grapes that he had shipped back east to sell to the Italians in our town who still made their own wine. And the past came back in a rush, those fall days my grandfather took me with him and my younger brother too: the boxes of grapes stacked in the open, orange doors of the railroad car; the car parked on a sidetrack until it could be unloaded; the men in shirtsleeves and hats tipped back who came to pick up their boxes of grapes, their voices rising in fragments of Italian and English; the thin cigars they smoked leaving a sweet, acrid scent in the air.

I liked going there—my grandfather handing us some grapes to eat, and the smell of the fruit in those cars, the sweet taste of the grapes, the afternoon sun casting its shadows around the freight car, the men talking, the trains pulling in at the station.

As I waited for my father, it all came back, and I felt the new kind of strength that had little to do with the military and more about my own decision to do what I'd done. Call it a new awareness of being alone with myself, a new inner determination. Even if enlisting had come with its consequences, it was my decision, a decision I made alone. When I saw my father's black Dodge pull into the parking lot, I knew he'd be alone. I knew my stepmother did not approve of my enlistment as if it were a sign that she had failed to raise me properly, as if I'd done something wrong again.

My father was glad to see me, but he was shocked to see the boot-camp haircut, the winter dress uniform. And he asked me about the train ride, the stopovers, the training we'd had after boot camp. At home nothing had changed. My brother was 14, just starting his first year of high school. When my parents asked me where I would be going next, I told them my orders were for the Marine Air Station in Cherry Point, North Carolina. It would be a long bus ride south. I had ten days' leave.

8. Here, There and Everywhere

Although I'd only been away those few months, things had changed in my hometown. The crowd I knew from high school had gone to college or to work. And when my friend Joe picked me up in his car and took me up to his home, the first guy I met on his street was Dave who had run track and cross country with me in high school.

When I tried to shake his hand, he hit me hard in the gut and was surprised that I didn't even flinch. In fact, he laughed. I'd been doing so many sit-ups since July, it didn't hurt.

Later, Joe and I met up with some of our old friends who were going to the local community college or working at the IBM plants downtown. We shared a few beers at a local place where they'd served us (as minors) in high school, and as I was still underage I couldn't get served even with my Marine ID. Those who had gone away to college, including my old girlfriend Bernadette, were still away at school.

I felt a sense of displacement, a distance from what my old friends were doing. The draft had just started up in November—not the lottery, but a regular draft. Some of the guys from high school had joined the reserves so they could stem the draft while they were in college.

~ ~ ~

At home, I got a few books to read and tried to get along with my family. In the quiet of my old room at night, I could feel a new kind of aloneness slip around me. Before I knew it, my leave was up. And all the way travelling back south again on the bus to North Carolina, I could feel that sense of being alone return. It was as if my uniform were part of the feeling—a deep look at what I'd wanted to do—get out, get away, leave my home behind. And I had accomplished this.

There was a good feeling that came with being alone too, but it took some getting used to—this new me, this stranger who watched the countryside go by—dark glimpses of Washington, D.C., and then Virginia. By early morning, we'd reached North Carolina.

I lasted four months at the Marine Air Station. After I was promoted to private first class and had been assigned every lousy detail

Part I—Marking Time

a "new guy" could get, including a three-week "exercise" guarding a deserted airstrip in the North Carolina outback and participating in "staged" combat patrols on that operation (with blanks); and after an older corporal had asked me to break his lower leg with a 2 × 4 on that same detail, with a promise to give me $50 (he was worried about going overseas); and after I told him I couldn't do it; and after the "simulated combat operation" ended and I was back in the barracks, I signed up for the first orders I saw posted on the HQ captain's wallboard of notices. The orders were for Chu Lai, Vietnam.

~ ~ ~

9

New Beginnings

It starts now in a different way—a new doctor, a therapist at the Bronx VA, someone to talk to for the first time in 50+ years. The letter I sent to the *New York Times* reads: "I enjoyed Kevin Powers' essay on Vonnegut's *Slaughterhouse-Five* in Sunday's Book Review. As a fellow veteran who has just entered VA treatment for PTSD after 50 years being unstuck in time, I feel a kinship to Billy Pilgrim. I was discharged from a locked ward of a Naval Hospital in 1968 after going AWOL from the Marines when I returned from Vietnam at 19. Like Vonnegut I too have raised my three sons to see beyond the 'self-deceptions' and outright lies that keep the war machine in business. And I am also grateful *Slaughterhouse-Five, or, The Children's Crusade* is still in print. Vonnegut's Mrs. O'Hare is right—we were all children when we went to war." And he's good, this Dr. Morley. He's not a psychiatrist—after a bunch of visits he tells me how the *body remembers* and I start to think that is why I'm hunched into my age—that my shoulders are taking it in—these fragmentary things, pieces of what has happened to me—of what I've seen.

He says there's a new theory spinning about PTSD, and that a moral compass plays into it. I mean, what you have seen can be amplified by what you know is wrong. And I'm thinking about this as I walk out through the doors—the vets in wheelchairs sitting outside in the shade and the late afternoon coolness settling in around them.

~ ~ ~

PART II
Going South

10

Standing in the Shadows of Love

There were many ways to die. You might die from heat exhaustion or heatstroke like Mike Woods and three others did on Operation Union II. You might die from falling off a radio tower in Thailand like Freddy D. who played football with you in high school. You might get dysentery and die bit by bit. You might get sick from food poisoning or from bad water.

You might get malaria or other bug-related sicknesses. You could be hurt and killed by one of your own vehicles like Don Harding who was crushed in the company yard by a deuce and a half truck. You could get an infection from a small cut and die from the spread of that infection.

You could die from drowning because you passed out and fell face first into water. You could die from exposure to DDT or defoliants, but usually that took longer. You could die by accident—a mortar round falling short of its mark. You might get shot by one of your own—a nervous new guy who didn't know what he was doing and who shot you in the back on a routine patrol.

That's the way PK went. You might get shelled by your own artillery and die from that. And yes, you could die from getting your foot punctured or tripping a booby trap—a land mine, a spiked grenade. And you could die in base camp asleep in your cot or in a town or a city from plastic explosives. You could die on guard duty or on a convoy or in the crash of a helicopter.

You could fall from a gunship, a moving truck, a watchtower. You could be shot in any number of ways and die out in the open or in the open doorway of a medevac chopper.

10. Standing in the Shadows of Love

    You could die in your sleep in a hospital tent or you could die wide awake in the arms of a friend or alone in the pit of some tunnel. You could make it all the way home whole and die in your car on a back road like Shaw did. You could OD and die in country or back in the world. You could get busted back home and die resisting arrest. You could get all the way stateside and commit suicide. You could die slowly each day back and drink yourself out. You could smoke dope and snort cocaine and hang yourself in the upstairs of your parents' house like Michaels did. You could die of wounds in a veterans' hospital 30 miles from your hometown.

    It was easy to die. Harder I think to stay alive, to add up the days on your short timer's stick—tick them off until you were almost there, but I didn't believe in counting down the days—and I never did. Then, on the night I was supposed to leave, the mortars and rockets fell on the airstrip shutting down the runways, keeping our freedom bird from making its landing. And watching the fire around the airstrip, feeling the shock of it, weaponless and in khakis instead of fatigues, we watched helpless as the night came on, slept curled up on our seabags in the open hangars.

~ ~ ~

11

Sunny

I remember the heat. Long shimmering waves of heat that took your breath away. I remember the dust rising off the runways and the noise of trucks and forklifts and planes taking off and landing. The heat came at you like a snarl and made you look up. It was hard to breathe. Soon my stiff, starched utility jacket was soaked through, the green undershirt they made me dye in Okinawa dark with sweat. Someone handed me a warm can of soda. A sergeant yelled for us to fall in, to listen for our names, to where we'd be going next.

Proctor and I got slips for a tent off the airstrip. Our planes

Okinawa, July 1966. Group shot of "new guys" (left to right): the author, PFC Proctor, PFC Montez, PFC Ramos, PFC Griggs.

11. Sunny

would take us north tomorrow or the next day. We walked inside the steel building and a driver came to take us to the temporary units. Proctor had this big knife he'd bought in one of the shops off the base in California. It had a 10-inch blade and a black sheath. *New guys*. We heard them say it. We couldn't see how we looked, how pale and clean and starched we were. It would take six months for us to see ourselves as we were then.

Now I think we were never 18. The years between then and now are not blurred or distant but seem like a quick glimpse backward, a glance over a shoulder. Maybe each of us who came overseas together knew separate wars, wars we witnessed alone.

I remember saying goodbye to Proctor the next morning when my flight north to Chu Lai was on the airfield. I never saw him again.

~ ~ ~

12

Chain of Fools

They called me Super Seal, short for *sealed beams*—the name of the headlights in our PC trucks and dump trucks, a take on the gray Marine-issue glasses I wore with thick plastic lenses. Puff, MD, tagged me.

I remember the first time he walked into our outfit after he'd deplaned. We were assembled for morning formation, standing at ease, waiting down for the man—our C.O. And then there he was, dragging his rear foot—steppin' down on us 'cause he knew we were watching, checking him out. A whisper ran through the assembled crew: *"Hey, dudes...."*

"It's MD, the Magic Dragon." And the name clung to him right then, or he to it. The good Doctor Feelgood. *MD*—the same dude really, or two dudes, two distinct rappers, making a play on all of us, on the place itself. And with the coming of MD, the place changed, got hazy or clearer, depending on who you were. For me, it was a way of finishing out and he saved it, made it smoother, hipper, slicker.

"That's one flying dude," Ward said, standing next to me. *"Check him out."*

The fingers of that giant hand that threatened to clutch at all of us didn't disappear but eked livable. You see, Puff's magic infected everyone, making the whole thing start to go dreamlike, like it would be dreamlike for the rest of our lives, like it would follow us and we it, while the world kept fouling us up, following us into everywhere we tried to hide or to reappear.

And from then on, the whole outfit started to lose it. Even the gunny (gunnery sergeant) in charge of the headquarters office got

12. Chain of Fools

loose. And in my last six months in country, I became the battalion scavenger.

After my first few runs into division HQ where I met some old high school friends who were working in the HQ office for the general, and where I managed to scrounge up some parts and office stuff for the gunnery sergeant, and where we made more contacts at other outfits too, the gunny started to like my new role as scrounger/thief. Things started to change, because if the gunny was happy he made sure everyone else was okay.

First, I went with just a truck and driver and we cruised other outfits and supply places. And after each ride, it got easier and I became more accustomed to the possibilities. I'd had a good teacher in Sgt. Bethlehem who had shown us how to manipulate situations, how to make something out of very little, how to trade off one item for another. Or as we called it *wheel and deal*.

In our battalion HQ, guys started strutting their stuff, bad-assing each other, learning to smooth talk and be cool from the brothers—drinking beer at the club at night, playing whist. There he is now, sidestepping his way through the hootch with some borrowed sergeant bars, and me pretending I'm a first lieutenant. MD gone into it, drawling, *"Just takin' care of my boys—you know,"* pointing to where PK and some of the others stood, watching Puff do the shuffle. *"What's the deal gonna be?"*

And through all the other nights too, making us pull together, keep on with the sky. As if the moon with its one good eye could bring us down or keep us from rapping, hoping to move through it all sideways too—smooth, too smooth for any of us. Puff, MD, the good Doctor Feelgood, making us believe we had a chance against time, against the things that were coming that we could not see.

~ ~ ~

13

Where Do We Go from Here?

Listen Bo—this was in the long ago and far away time when people fell from the sky and oily fire ate the days and nights. Some of us remember. Now there are only the ghosts who come back in the wet mornings when the dew rises off the grass and the open fields. There are many ghosts—wisps of tiny things that drift off and do not linger. It's the shadows you have to be on the lookout for—the shadows have ways of tripping you up. You have to listen to the empty spaces between the shadows, you have to look up into the light. It's easy for me, easy to see between the shadows—to look over into the dark and watch those will-o'-the-wisps come in to feed. They feed on dreams, man. Your dreams. My dreams.

I know, you're saying I'm incoherent—I'm old. I'm pulling into the deep side of things and my age shows. I'm walking the shadow line out into the night's coolness. I am. I am. But hang out for a while. Have a beer or two, some wine?

Smoke if you got 'em—the smoking lamp is lit. Sit down, I need to tell it right, you dig? I need to tell it again so you can understand.

In the late fall, the monsoon began and guys started coming over in twos or threes; one dude came over in just two days from Boston. Office guy with a briefcase full of socks and shirts—no overseas stuff, still so new you could smell the states on him and his smokes were freshly bought. He pulled the night guard with me first night he got in.

Picone. Don Picone. Crazy. Didn't know where we were. Even let the 2nd lieutenant of the guard sneak up on us until I heard that redneck out there and let my rifle bolt drop. And he stopped pretty quick—then I challenged him.

13. Where Do We Go from Here?

They called this new guy Pepe. He was okay though—the captain had him right up next to his desk for two weeks. The captain was a double D asshole. TJ Burke—a chickenshit captain with a red face. Even the gunny knew he was nickel dime. We had all kinds of names for the captain and there was no money on his head—he was just 10–58 as we called it then—out of service, done. Chrome dome was the best of all of the nicknames and he earned it.

There was a time when the youngest of us, the most naïve you might say, would dance with each other in the thatched roof hut they called our enlisted man's club. It's true, you dig, and the brothers started it—Lewis and Ward, Winston and Greer and some of the others. They knew TK and me we'd be down with it, but even some of the other white guys would pull into it. Listen, it was just us you see, the guys who didn't get it—who didn't know enough about anything. Eighteen or nineteen. Too stupid to know. We were free because we liked each other and we were in love with the moment. The bad things had not begun yet. The monsoon had not started. No one was hitting on Park Lanes or drinking hard stuff. It was early—or maybe it was late—depending on how you called it. Even the old gunny sergeant and Gramps started in to dancing one night. It was always the soul music—Impressions with Mayfield, Mary Wells, Smoky Robinson, Four Tops or Temptations. You had to lean into the sound you see, get your shoulders down, your hips moving and get down into it. Took a while for the gray boys like me and TK. But we got there. We made the deal. The old timers, white or Black, would scowl at us from the corners of the joint, nursing their beers and smoking cigarettes, but we didn't care about them. For us, the music was a way to forget where we were, to forget the things that had sent us there—and it was good music to dance to because dancing was a way of letting go. I know I'm flashing back. I know. But stay with me. Hold on.

You probably want to know how I ended up here. That's not hard to tell—I got the kick, you see, a month and change in the slammer and then it's a mental ward. But I'm getting ahead of myself, I'm jumping to the home front when I should stay in country. It starts with Boyd and Bullsan and Sergeant Bethlehem.

It's the HQ cook's tent where the head mess sergeant SSgt. Milton

Part II—Going South

Chu Lai, late summer 1966. Three members of Sgt. Bethlehem's 40 Thieves (left to right): the author, Alvarez, Morro.

used to listen to his Nancy Wilson tapes. He had it all, nice fans—a real floor. He'd hand you a cold beer and ask what you brought for him—contraband, Stolen stuff, things he could trade. We'd go there at dusk after he'd made the last meal. Man, it was hot—so hot then I kept sweating through my green tees until they rotted right off me. Milton would laugh at us—he'd call us the 40 Thieves because we were all waiting on orders then, and doing whatever they made us do. Opening boxes, loading stuff. They were long, hard days. There's more to it.

~ ~ ~

14.

Have You Ever Seen the Rain?

After I was transferred to the 1st Engineer Battalion, a few miles from FLSG-Bravo, where I'd spent eight weeks unloading cargo off ships, one thing that happened was the captain in charge of HS Company confronted me about talking to the Vietnamese children who hung around the entrance to our battalion's compound.

They were the only Vietnamese I'd met—and they were friendly—hoping we would buy some tin-backed mirrors (made out of old beer cans or Ho Chi Minh sandals cut from tires) or soft drinks, or trinkets—beads and souvenirs. They were just children. Captain T.E. Bloom was better known to us as "Chrome dome," a name derived from the nasty silver helmets they made us wear in boot camp. His nickname came from his bald head and his strange "spaceman"-like pale color—whenever it was hot and humid, like most of the time, the captain's face would turn a pale shade of red and his bald head would glow when he took off his utility cap. And that's how he got the tag *Chrome dome* Bloom, among many other four-letter asides.

When I turned my back on the Dome, he lost his cool. He yelled at me and ordered me to return and stand in front of him. Instead, I said, "Bullshit," and pushed out through the door of his office into the company area. By then, Captain Bloom was crazy angry and ordered the gunnery sergeant in charge of headquarters—a quiet new guy named Taylor—to place me under custody for insubordination and refusal to follow a direct order.

Gunnery Sgt. Taylor obeyed. And on that early fall day, I found myself on the way to the major in charge of the 1st Combat Engineer

Part II—Going South

Battalion, Major Ward—a seasoned major who'd been in the Korean War and was known as a good guy with always something nice to say to everyone. He smoked cigars and had that tough, weathered look of someone who knew the score, someone who had come up the hard way. And one guy he really hated was Captain Bloom. He knew Bloom was chickenshit, and a pain-in-the-ass, but he also knew I was a mere lance corporal, still only 18 years old—and he had to give me a serious dressing down. When he was done, he kind of smiled at me and asked what I wanted—and was not happy when I asked for a hearing. He could see I didn't want to back down. I lost. The major hit me with a pay reduction, battalion special duty, and loss of rank if I did not succeed in my special assignments.

This would last for at least a month.

The first detail was to accompany Corporal Jack "the Jip" Jones on his duties—these included dump runs, laundry runs, and more. The first time we went to the local village of Anton—where I had never been before—Jack ordered me to drop the laundry at the Vietnamese hut where they did our laundry and then get back in the PC to wait for him, as he had "some special stuff" to take care of, "y'know." I didn't know. I was still naïve about what went down in the village outside our compound. Fifteen or twenty minutes later, Jip came back with his twisted kind of grin. *"Next time you can get some too, Mac. Boom, Boom."* He laughed.

And then I realized the tin-roofed hut across the street was also where a teenage girl was being "forced" to prostitute herself for 10 dollars of military scrip a throw. I saw her come out into the doorway when the PC was pulling away. Jones had been her first "customer" of the day. Before that, I had never been in a "Ville" before. I was almost three months in country and most of the time at FLSG-Bravo we just worked 10- or 12-hour days in the open yards unloading boxes of gear and supplies. Once or twice, I rode guard in an open truck to escort a "new guy" to a grunt outfit off Highway One. And things had been bad that past summer of 1966, the line outfits had taken heavy casualties still running the old search and destroy patrols—none of which were paying off. Forty percent casualties. And I felt bad for that new guy as he jumped down off the back of the truck, shouldering his

14. Have You Ever Seen the Rain?

gear and his rifle. And I thought about my own luck, about how a few nights back—the sarge would not let me volunteer for transfer to a line outfit—when a call came out for volunteers. He saw me standing outside in the dim light of early evening and said, *"You ain't goin' nowhere, Mac. All you guys are getting transferred soon enough, so get your butt back to the tent and hit the rack."* No one argued with Sgt. Bethlehem.

It felt strange now, doing these details with Jack. The next one was the dump run, and I wasn't prepared for this one either. This time we picked up all the mess hall slop, 30-gallon drums of wasted food from the previous night's dinner and the morning and lunch of the present day—drums full of coffee grounds and wasted food—at least 10 drums in all. And the detail was to empty those drums and return to the base. What I didn't know then—but found out much later on—was that it was common to do what Jack did that day. Years later, I tried to write a poem about it before I knew it was common practice.

~ ~ ~

Here's the poem:

>At the garbage dump—the air fills with flies
>you hear the droning sigh
>above the truck's motor—
>the cries of children
>fighting for scraps of food, leftovers
>tin cans, mess hall waste—
>Jack laughs, pushes the 30-gallon drum
>toward the tailgate.
>The children shout
>surge toward us.
>Watch this, he says,
>tipping the drum on its side,
>it splashes down, covering them
>in coffee grounds, stale bread,
>egg shells.

To Corporal Jack, it was funny. I never forgot it. And then many years later, I read in the Winter Soldier Investigation that this was a common thing to do—to dump our garbage and make a game of

Part II—Going South

it—letting it splash down on those who came to get it, those who were hungry enough to eat what we threw away. I only made this run once. My next assignments were guard duty and kitchen duty, and more. It lasted for three weeks, and then the gunnery sergeant told me I had to come back—we were going to move to Danang in a month or so and it would be my job to help us organize the move. We had to go by ship since Highway One was still not safe for convoys of trucks.

15

Darkness, Darkness

The day the comm guys brought the two prisoners up to battalion HQ, I was working in the yards. I watched them come up the dirt road on a *Mule*—a six-foot platform truck—official nomenclature: U.S. Military M274 Truck, Platform, Utility ½ Ton, 4 × 4. It was odd to see the two prisoners strapped to the rails. They seemed so small next to the driver and the corporal who was guarding them. I had never seen *the enemy* before and the two black-haired men looked more like children. They seemed young and scared and I could sense their fear as the driver slammed the vehicle to a halt and they were thrown forward.

"Stay the fuck back!" the corporal yelled at me.

I had been three months in country then. Two months at a supply dump called FLSG-Bravo tucked onto the cliffs near the South China Sea and then another month and change at 1st Combat Engineers out near the end of the airstrip near Tam Ky, though the village we were closest to was called Anton.

I will never forget those two men—Vietnamese civilians suspected of collaborating with the enemy or of being them. Seeing those two suspected VC close up made the war we were waging there seem close up too. I saw those two men chained to the *Mule* and for those few moments they were just men—scared and small, looking as if they didn't trust us or the place they'd been brought to by the corporal. They were men after all, farmers from the village below our compound. And they worked, I could see the work in their hands, and in the way they gripped the rails so they could hold on to the sides of that rig as the driver pulled into the yard. They wanted to have some dignity—so as not to appear the way the guys wanted them to appear.

Part II—Going South

Chu Lai, fall 1966. author, 1st Engineer Battalion, in the monsoon rain.

 I don't know what happened to them—whether they were found to be VC collaborators or not or where they were taken to after they left our outfit. Nothing outside of the battalion HQ was secure. The Viet Cong let us believe we held the high ground when in fact we held nothing at all except the barbed-wire perimeter around our outfit. When we left in early March to move to Danang, the army units that moved into our compound got hit immediately. It was as if the enemy were trying to tell them something about who was in control, about what was important.

~ ~ ~

16

Who'll Stop the Rain?

After Puff gave me the name Super Seal, the gunnery sergeant in charge of the headquarters and supply office asked if he got me a truck and driver could I get some wooden pallets for our heavy equipment platoon—we needed places to store motors and engine parts for our forklifts and dump trucks ... there was no place to keep the things dry and secure. I told him I'd give it a try if he let me take along at least one other man. On this first trip, Puff took the ride with me and the driver and we headed toward the Danang supply yards.

That first trip proved fortuitous in many ways. As we were driving around the yards at the Marine supply central in Danang, we kept running into MPs who asked for our papers. Getting out of the rig to show one of them the orders, I heard someone call out my name: *"Mac—Hey, Mac!"*

And standing there by the supply depot was Jim Murray, a kid I knew from the Marine Air Wing at Cherry Point, North Carolina—the outfit they'd sent me to after boot camp and advanced training and where I'd shipped out from on my way to California and *points south*.

He was laughing, and then suddenly another guy from the old airwing crew showed up, McGinty, both of them laughing and joking and telling me:

"Hey, we thought you were dead, dude, we thought you'd been killed."

It turned out they'd shipped out together and got the same gig in Danang near the airfield—unloading cargo. We got the pallets, 20 or 30 of them ... and then as were about to leave, they asked, *"You need some juice?"*

Part II—Going South

Sure, I said—knowing they meant POM juice—a product we could sell to the other guys in the battalion. McGinty had a forklift driver load a full pallet of juice on our truck—over 40 cases of juice.

"You don't have a typewriter lying around?" I asked. *"I would sure like one for the gunnery sergeant who runs the office at HQ."* And Jim just laughed, handed us a few beers and in a few minutes a PFC showed up with a typewriter—the large office type with a cover.

And in my last months in country, I became the battalion scavenger. My outfit cut me out of night guard and any other duties—and because I was *short,* because I'd be going home—they let me steal or scavenge whatever we needed. In May, the guys in the heavy equipment platoon and motor transport needed wheel cylinders and brake shoes. We'd been burning up both in the mud and rains, so they sent me back to Chu Lai near the ocean to scavenge what I could. I knew the crew back there in Chu Lai. The outfit was FLSG-Bravo and had been my first outfit when I deplaned and stumbled into the war.

The HQ captain gave me a pass to get me on a plane south to the Marine base at Chu Lai. I don't remember how I got to the base from the air station, and I don't remember how it all went down, but I got the wheel cylinders and some brake shoes too and other things the heavy equipment guys needed. My mail sack was full.

I spent the night in a tent on an empty cot, and I talked with the guys who had stayed behind there, still unloading cargo boxes and shipping containers. Flying back on another C-130 prop plane, I thought about my old outfit, about what had changed there and what was still the same. Some of the crew were still there: Boyd and the new sarge who had taken Sgt. Bethlehem's place. Except for a couple of transfers, I was alone on the plane going back. The transfers—some guys going to the 1st Marine Headquarters in Danang—wanted to know what I had in the mail sack and couldn't believe it was wheel cylinders, brake shoes and parts for our heavy forklifts and graders. They didn't understand we needed those things and couldn't get them via the regular supply channels.

This flight on a C-130 was a strange one. No one could believe that we needed those parts so badly they'd cut me orders to go back to Chu Lai to scrounge the parts. There was no order we could fill—I

16. Who'll Stop the Rain?

Danang, spring 1967. Three friends who helped scrounge the things we needed (left to right): Ward, Turner, Louis.

had to get the guys I knew from before to agree to give me the wheel cylinders and brake shoes and whatever else they could spare. I had the part numbers since they were specific to our vehicles. And we could never get them in Danang. Boyd and one of the new guys helped me out. It was tricky, the new sarge had no clue as to why I was there, but he saw I had legitimate orders, so he went about his own duties.

I must have hitchhiked to the airport both ways because no one picked me up. I know I hadn't been issued a .45 caliber pistol, so I must have carried that leather mail sack and my M-14 with one 20-round magazine. Awkward, but that had to be the case. Now what I remember was the flight to Chu Lai and back, tied into the cargo netting and feeling the plane vibrate as it took off with its big empty belly and a few soldiers belted into the makeshift seats. For me it was kind of a strange two days, floating back and forth from two bases alone and on my own.

And those runs continued. Most of the time, it was a scrounge

Part II—Going South

Danang, summer 1967. LCpl Louis and two Vietnamese girls are selling trinkets in Danang City during our scrounging run.

run, a "get what you can" kind of thing, and I usually took at least one friend with me if they were free. The gunny didn't care and he cleared it with Chrome dome who had faded into a kind of slump and just left us alone. Things were popping in Danang, and now A Company had moved north toward the DMZ. That left B and C Companies behind with us in Danang. And soon Braxton, the battalion armorer, said he was going to Cambodia to bring the new M-16s to the crew from A Company who had been sent there to assist other infantry outfits. He actually asked me to come along and ride shotgun with him, but the gunny said I was needed in Danang. And I knew he had other things he wanted me to acquire if I could. It was May 1967. I'd made E-4 in April, so I was now a corporal and officially an NCO.

~ ~ ~

17

Carry That Weight

"One needs a town, if only for the pleasure of leaving it," Cesare Pavese wrote in his novel *La Luna e il Falo* (The Moon and the Bonfire). And he goes further, "A town means not being alone, knowing that in the people, the trees, the soil, there is something of yourself and that even when you're not there, it stays and waits for you."

I know I left my own town for the first time when I was seventeen, and when I came back after being away for almost a year and a half, many things were different, and I had changed, even though the place and the feel of the place had not. I remember that first homecoming from war and the anticipation I felt about it. Now I understand that enlisting in the Marines was a foolish and spontaneous kind of thing to do, yet it accomplished what I had wanted by putting a real distance between myself and the place—the town, the streets where I'd grown up—and those childhood trials and failures did not feel as important as they once had.

They had slipped into the past like the old clothes in my room and like the room itself with its twin single beds and the guardian angel picture on the wall, the wooden crucifix next to it with the holy oil inside; there seemed a distance, the room and all the nights I'd spent there, reading books under the blankets by flashlight, falling asleep to the sound of cars on the road outside.

Now what comes back is how brief that first homecoming from Vietnam was, how really insignificant and small my town felt, yet I knew there was still something of myself there I wanted to revisit, a part of my own growing up that was lost to me and I would never get back. Even after all these years, I still remember the cool morning, the shade of the trees along the streets, the stillness and quiet.

Part II—Going South

And when the cab driver pulled away out of the driveway, I felt a new awareness I'd never recognized before. It had been a long series of rides, and most of them unpleasant and tedious. And the long bus ride up from New York City was no different, except this time in my summer uniform of wrinkled khakis I knew I'd been lucky.

And I remembered the other stopovers—the flight to El Toro, California, the ride to the airport in Los Angeles, and then JFK in New York—where all the flights had been cancelled for the night, so that I signed on for a six-hour bus ride upstate on a Trailways—a trip that made frequent stops at small towns all along the route to Binghamton. And then the cab ride to my father's house on West Main in Endicott. The old maples still lined the streets then—the GI homes built after World War II.

I remember the cool, early morning ride through my hometown, the summer smells of honeysuckle and the deep green scent of the maples. I saw how small my father's house was, how different it seemed from before I'd gone away. My parents were just getting up—when I rang the back-door bell, they were surprised to see me—surprised because there was no way to let them know when I'd be back. Pay phones were the only option then, and I had not wanted to miss my bus upstate—the midnight bus and the last one until late the next morning.

That homecoming seemed to me then and now an artificial one; coming home from the war that summer of 1967 seemed different because I had been away since early May of 1966, first to California for special training and then on to Tokyo and Okinawa before going "south" as we called it then—the flight to Vietnam. And looking back was a bittersweet task that came with the ride back. Call it growing up if you can believe that at 19, I was feeling that—a sense of being on my own with a surety of purpose and a new aloneness that made me call a cab to drive me back home—smoking a cigarette, the dark tan of my face and arms standing out against the summer khaki uniform—a stewardess at JFK touching my shoulder—*"Hey, good to see those ribbons"*—campaign ribbons pinned above the pocket of my shirt, a sure sign of where I'd been.

You come home alone and no one knows what it's like. For me

17. Carry That Weight

there was a kind of grace in it—a light that made me remember why I had left home in the first place—the arguments, the small town with nowhere to go, the feeling that leaving was the only way to shed the skin of childhood. Although alone is the truth, more alone than I'd ever felt before. And this time the aloneness would not let go of me, it clung like a mist or a shadow, and I couldn't shake it. I felt like there was a stranger in the room, someone I hardly knew—and the stranger was me. Alone, aloof, apart. It stayed and grew and became my "thing" and I could not shake it or find a way out of the despair and unrest it brought.

~ ~ ~

18

Slippin' into Darkness

I was arrested by the local police on a warm July night two days after I came back from my 13-month tour of duty. The charges were assault, interference with a senior police officer in the line of duty, disturbing the peace, and disorderly conduct. At the time of my arrest, I was wearing dark shades, camouflage shorts, a dark blue T-shirt and a button-front sweater in spite of the heat—70 degrees felt cold to me after all those months in a country with temps of 120 degrees.

The camo shorts I got from a Korean Marine or ROC as we called them. I'd traded him my pilot's survival knife for the shorts. We'd met at China Beach three weeks before I left for the states. It was the summer of 1967. Three of my friends who were not in the military also got arrested with me that night, but because I was still on active duty and only home for 20 days I was in trouble with the commanding officer at my new duty station: a naval weapons facility in the swamps outside of Charleston, South Carolina, where my job specialty would now be to guard the bunkers where Polaris missiles were kept.

As we waited in the small police station for my friend Don's father to come to bail us out, I started to see the trip coming home that summer. It was a long seam of journeys—first from Danang to Okinawa, and the four days we spent there getting processed out and picking up our gear we'd stored there. I thought about the seabags no one would claim, the ones belonging to the guys who did not make it back, those bags tagged and numbered and piled in the Quonset huts. I wondered about those seabags. What happened to the bags that were unclaimed—were they sent home? Or did some remain there?

18. Slippin' into Darkness

The second night back one of my friends threw a party for me in the garage of his father's home on the street behind our house. They had a keg of beer and *speidies*—lamb marinated and cut into chunks for cooking on an open fire—a local specialty brought in by the Italian workers who had come to work in the shoe factories. Eventually, the talk got around to what had been happening in Newark and Rochester and other places. Don, one of my old friends from high school, had been to college at R.I.T. in Rochester and everyone had an opinion on what those "Black people" should be doing.

I tried to say something about my outfit in Vietnam, how I'd gotten to know some soul brothers there pretty well and for the first time in my life had begun to understand a few things about racism and prejudice. Right off, I knew it was the wrong thing to say. They didn't get it. Now I know there was no way they could get it. We'd grown up in a working-class town—a town where there were no Black people.

It was ethnically diverse since the shoe factories employed workers from Italy, Greece, Poland, Russia and Czechoslovakia. But except for small enclaves of African Americans in the sister towns north of ours, we were "white." I dropped what I was going to say about those race riots in Rochester and Detroit and Newark, about how they were justified, about the need to break free of the stupid notions we'd all been raised to believe, and I had some beer, ate some of the good food and avoided talking about the war and about how I felt. Later that night we all went up to the north side of town, the Italian side, and "hung out" where everyone went in those days. The old crowd from high school was still there, going to college or working in the plants downtown instead of the shoe factories. Time seemed to stand still.

Instead of 1967, it felt as if it were 1963 or earlier and the world I'd seen was tucked out of sight, hidden by the factories, the parks, the well-kept lawns, the hills above the town that made the valley below seem even more redolent and green. Our arrest that night was just a fluke. Four of us were in the wrong place at the wrong time, and when the police tried to arrest my friend Pat, I spoke up, got involved and that's all it took.

Waiting in the police station, I remembered how it had started.

Part II—Going South

Coming back was a series of encounters, of images. When the motor pool guys told me I'd have to wait for the battalion driver, I just looked at them.

"Think I'll try to hitch a ride with one of the trucks from the 1st Marines, if that's ok with you."

"You're already out," the dispatcher said. "You can do what the fuck you wanna do."

I hitched a ride in the back of an empty PC that was going toward the airstrip. Now I can still see those villages go by, the tin-roofed huts, the children watching us, the smell of smoke from cooking fires, the smells of food. And beyond those huts along the road, those Vietnamese villagers we'd come to know in the last few months. You have to look back even after all this time, you need to see the landscape again. The sweet smell of flowers and the deep green of trees in the late morning heat and the dust kicking up behind us like a smudge of memory.

~ ~ ~

My father gave me the local newspaper article about the arrest that night. He saved it for me.

"The Chief of Police, D. Promide said there were arrests for interference with and assault on a police officer, disorderly conduct, public intoxication, and disturbing the peace."

Part III
Nothing for Nothing

19

Four Days Gone

It's a rainy early spring afternoon and my son Nate and I are driving home from his dental appointment. He's been listening to a song about a soldier who refused orders to return to Iraq. It's by *State Radio/Dispatch* and the song is called "Camilo." The soldier's name is Camilo Mejia. Nate has just turned 18 and he knows I was in the Marines and had some trouble after coming back from Vietnam. And although I never did what Camilo did, he knows I did some time in a civilian jail and military brigs.

Today he wants to know about what happened to me when I turned away from the Marine Corps after my tour in Vietnam. He wants to know about the consequences. He wants the details. It seems appropriate to be driving in a car since a car was how I made my getaway the first time I ever broke the rules. And I tell him right off, *"I'm no Camilo. What I did was different and the deal was different, too."*

"What do you mean?" he asks. "What happened to you when you deserted? What did they do to you?"

And I try to explain to him that although I was *listed* as a deserter, in fact, if you turn yourself in, in uniform, they eventually drop the desertion charge. I try and tell him how it started, turning away from the military, taking flight and going AWOL (Absent Without Official Leave) from the Marine Corps, but instead I see the Monday morning when I turned myself in to the FBI office in Binghamton, New York. A winter morning, two days past Christmas. Snow clouds overhead and the gray stillness of the winter morning. My parents dropping me off in front and driving away. I'm carrying my seabag and the envelope with the DD 553 the Marine Corps

19. Four Days Gone

sent to my home address—the form indicating I was now listed as a deserter. I remember climbing the stone stairs looking for the right office. The door ajar, the agent looking up at me as I knocked.

But my son wants to know about consequences, and he wants to know why. And I go back to the Marine Barracks/Sea School in Norfolk, Virginia. I go back to the day I reported late for duty.

As I try to explain, I realize it's no good, I can't tell him what it was like being alone and not knowing what to do, I can't even tell him why I did it. Spur of the moment, walking out of the barracks down there in Virginia. Unlike Camilo, I didn't know what I was doing or why I was doing it. Yet, even today, all these years later, all I know is I had to do it. I had to get out. I can't tell him it was for a reason, for a cause, for an awakening. It wasn't political. Or maybe "we have to unlearn things." I think that is it, really. Yet, all these years later, all I know is I was compelled to turn away from the Marines, from what I had been doing for over two years.

And then I try to tell him about waiting—I had to stand in a hallway while I waited for the 1st sergeant to see me. When you're late in the military they call it AWOL. My leave had expired after three days and then I was supposed to report for training. So technically I was on the fence, they could call it AWOL or they could just let it go.

It was Sea School—dress blues, sword drills, rifle drills, spit and polish nonsense. Once you complete the course of study there, you are assigned a ship and become part of the detachment of Marines on that vessel. And they'd given me three days to get from Charleston, South Carolina, to Virginia, without going home. I was less than two months back from my 13-month tour in Vietnam.

And for the first time in my short two years as a Marine, I decided to say no—a mistake any way you cut it in the Marine Corps. A double mistake if you are an NCO—a corporal up for promotion to sergeant. And in my 19 years, I had never turned away from an assignment or a set of orders. As I waited for *the first shirt* (the 1st sergeant), the PFC on duty took my orders and looked up from his desk.

"You're late," he said, *"three days late."*

In the few minutes following the office guy's quip, I made the

Part III—Nothing for Nothing

decision. And I tell Nate—who loves music, loves to sing and write songs, loves to play music and listen to all kinds of music—*Well, there was no music in those hallways, only the stagnant decaying silence, and the creak of footsteps on passageways, a distant echo of boots and someone outside counting cadence. Nothing but those cases of swords, old dress blue uniforms preserved under glass—relics of past sea-going Marines, the dead air of polished wood floors, the creeping silence of time standing still, a past that was gone and could never be any more than a window on another time, the burnt-out ash of faded glory and old lies.*

Then, without thinking of the consequences, without thinking I'd already turned in my orders, because if I'd thought about it, without my orders they wouldn't have found out about me for months.

I told the clerk I was going to the "head" (Marine/Navy jargon for the bathroom) and instead I pushed out through the door and walked quickly to my car in the parking lot. I kept thinking they'd be after me, they'd be stopping me. But no one did. The gate guard waved me through and I drove toward downtown Norfolk to hock what personal stuff I had with me for gas money. At a gas station restroom, I changed into civilian clothes—blue jeans and a T-shirt. Now, there was no turning back.

And I try to tell Nate how it began—the transfer, the new duty station. My friend DeCarlo and I had both applied for orders; we both agreed we had to do something to get out of the swamps and the Naval Weapons Station in Charleston where we'd been stationed when we came back from the war. Our jobs had been as security guards for the Polaris missiles entombed in bunkers throughout the base.

"Fuckin' ass MPs," DeCarlo had said. And we were. Except we were guards with Top Secret clearances. Soldiers with responsibilities.

We would drive pickups at night to check the bunkers or stand gate guard duty during the days. We had to check the IDs of all incoming personnel. DeCarlo said a full-bird colonel, checking to see if the sentry was with it, that colonel had flashed an ID with a dog's face where the mug shot was supposed to be. The sentry had let him pass without checking it. Then they'd busted the dude down to

19. Four Days Gone

private. There was also a story about a lance corporal who had gone crazy late at night at one of the substation checkpoints and began to shoot out the windows of the guard booth with his .45-caliber pistol. The shots were reported by other sentries, and eventually the sergeant of the guard had to come and take the guy away. Another story was about a Marine in his pickup who'd driven into a bunker where the missiles were. He thought he'd seen a covered wagon on the road. The base had that effect on you. Live oaks with moss hanging down, swamp gas, giant snakes lying across the roads.

And there were ghosts out there—the place had a history, you know, old rice plantations, slave quarters. You'd get to thinking about haints; the stumps on the sides of the roads looming up like bits of those who had been there before us, shards of broken dreams rising in the rain and mist. At night alone in your truck, doing the checkpoints, you started to see the shadows had depth, and sometimes you stopped your truck short and just stared out at the road ahead, the headlights illuminating those shadows, bringing the night in close.

So DeCarlo, who had been a truck driver and mechanic in Vietnam, suggested we put in for orders out of there, the first orders that came up. DeCarlo got 8th and I in Washington, D.C., better known as the President's Own. And I got Sea School. Now, listening to my son ask me about the day I walked away from the Marines—the day I decided not to wait for the 1st sergeant and the day I officially became AWOL and then after another 60 days, a deserter—I keep seeing the morning I turned myself in to the authorities.

~ ~ ~

The agent looks up at me, surprised to see me in my winter dress uniform with the campaign ribbons over the breast pocket, indicating I've been in Vietnam.

I'm not scared, I'm just wondering *Okay, what next?* I have that deep sinking feeling in my gut—this was not going to turn out well. I hand him the envelope with the form and he reads it and says:

"Hey, I can't take you today. Let's go see if the Marine Corps recruiter wants you."

And we walk back down two flights to the Marine recruiter's

Part III—Nothing for Nothing

office, both of them talk for a while, and the recruiter decides he'll take me up to the Marine Reserve Station near Tully, New York, and see if they will hold me there.

"*Let the reservists do something',*" he says. "*They don't do shit as it is.*"

And I see the drive north again, the car moving through the snow squall, the recruiter up in front and me sitting next to him. And I want to tell Nate about that ride, about the car and how it felt to be alone with the recruiter.

"*You can smoke if you got 'em,*" he says.

I'm still smoking Kools then and I light up. The menthol rush comes on with the snow falling against the car windows. It's an old government Ford Galaxy and the windshield wipers are vacuum jobs that are tied to a pump. I hear the slapping noise they make as the snow gets going. There's a grayness all around, a dull gray color to the sky like old clay—so you know it's going to snow some more, that upstate snow that swirls at you and you get to seeing other things, you get to remember.

And even now it still comes back, the noise of the tires on the pavement, the roster of the names of towns we pass—Whitney Point, Marathon, Homer, Catullus, Tully. And when we get to the Marine Reserve Station, the warrant officer there—a short, stubby guy with a midday shadow of a shave and a tuft of dark brown hair—shakes his head. "*What the hell's this, now, hey?*"

He takes the papers from the recruiter and brings me into his office, kind of snorts and then gets serious.

"*We shouldn't be taking you in at all,*" he says. "*An NCO and a vet to boot. You should have gone back on your own. But I can't let you do that now. Now we gotta take you to the civvie jail in Syracuse. Onondaga County. Then you wait for the chasers to take you downstate.*"

And he tells me, "*When you finally get back remember this—it's wrong and it'll work for you when you go for the hearing. This ain't legal. It's wrong under the UCMJ Code.*"

I'm listening, but outside the station I hear the wind pick up. And two six-foot privates in MP gear and .45-caliber pistols in

19. Four Days Gone

holsters come in and get on either side of me. They point me to the door and walk me out to another gray Ford.

An older sergeant is driving and the two mugs sit on either side of me in the back seat—and then they pull out their .45s to let me know they mean business. I kind of smile when they do that—the sarge is watching me in the rearview mirror, and he tells the two to holster their weapons. They've never been anywhere—just reservists who want to play it up, pretend they're tough guys.

It's still snowing when we get to the jail in Syracuse. The escorts leave me with the jailer and he leads me upstairs. I have to walk past all the cells in the block in my uniform, and I'm aware of the other inmates' stares—my dress greens, the overseas campaign ribbons. Probably a good thing too, just to keep some distance. I spent almost two weeks in that jail waiting for Marine brig chasers to come up from New York City. There were other soldiers there who had to be escorted downstate too, guys who were running away from the war.

I'd never been in handcuffs before or jail either and so the idea of being cuffed and sitting between those two reservist guards made the deserter tag seem real for the first time, and it made the act of leaving Norfolk that day in late September seem real, too.

~ ~ ~

And walking out past the clerk before the 1st sergeant could talk to me, getting into the car and driving out past the gate guard who just flagged me through, hocking my watch in a downtown pawnshop for gas money, changing out of my uniform into blue jeans and a T-shirt in a gas station men's room—all of it comes back again and again.

I tell Nate, *"Well, I just left. I'd had enough of it, you know."*

And I think that's close to the truth, but I'm leaving things out on purpose. I'm leaving out the nightmares, the waking sweats. Now I could tell him more, I could try to explain what it was like, or maybe give him the James Jones line about *knowing my luck had run out and I'd never make it through another tour*—whether it was Sea School first or not—I knew they'd be sending me back overseas. But that wouldn't be the truth, because I would have gone back to my old

Part III—Nothing for Nothing

outfit in Vietnam, or even another outfit; there was something we had there together that was honest and true.

And I was still too naïve then to realize what we were doing in Vietnam was wrong; it would take a couple more years for me to wake up to the truths of that war—the stupid, cruel truths I had witnessed and that would take the lives of so many.

~ ~ ~

And I'm not telling him about the flashbacks, about the dead, about the other stuff. I'm deliberately not telling Nate how it had come to this, how the story really started. I can't really see things like that anymore—nothing is one dimensional.

Instead, I tell him about the day I was finally discharged, about getting out of the hospital and taking a cab to the airport, about the riots in Norfolk and Portsmouth—the bus station closed, the trains not running. It was April 9, 1968, the day they buried Martin Luther King.

He doesn't want to know about this—he wants to know about punishment, about what happened when I got back to the base in Norfolk. And yet, as he sits there across from me, I'm seeing the snow again, the day they took us out of that jail in Syracuse to the airport to ride on the Mohawk prop plane to New York.

Slowhawk, we called it. This time they had an official MP escort—three lance corporals and a sergeant. The sergeant handcuffed me by myself. The others were handcuffed together. There were five of us in all. Four guys running away from the war and me. The sergeant wanted to know what I was doing there, and in uniform. He couldn't figure it out.

It was mid–January—another gray day with no sun. Standing in the airport waiting room in Syracuse, we must have been a sight. The four guys in civvies and me in my dress greens. The guy next to me named Mel wanted to make a break for it. *"Where would we go?"* I asked. Staring out at the runways it seemed like a bleak prospect, and besides I'd turned myself in. I told him I had to go on with it. There was nothing else.

Then there was the Brooklyn Naval Yard in January snow—the

19. Four Days Gone

Brooklyn Brig where we half-stepped to chow in a brig shuffle, the line when we checked in to be interviewed, searched, given brig haircuts, remembering my own intake—

"What you readin' there, Corporal shit-bird, what the fuck is this?"

The thick paperback was stuffed in my shaving kit. *Letting Go.* The corporal read the title and smiled.

"Can't have no fuckin' books in here, asshole." He threw it on the pile of "contraband" behind him. *"Can't have comic books, or fuck books, or any kind of books."* He smiled again, almost a leer.

"You won't be needing this steel comb either," he said. *"You some kinda reader, Corporal shit-bird, motherfucker? Huh? You some fuckin' smartass? Gotta get your hair cut, too. First thing you dudes is gonna do is see the barber. All right, move out."*

When I got to the barrack room of the brig, my seabag had been tagged and stored and I had been issued a wool blanket and a towel.

"Move out, move out," the guards kept shouting.

I stumbled into the bunk area and the others there looked up at me.

~ ~ ~

And my son has me remembering the trip north after I first left Virginia—the early fall day I drove all the way from Norfolk, Virginia, to upstate New York on less than 20 dollars. One of the rear tires in my 1961 Chevy Impala coupe kept going soft and I had to stop every hundred miles or so to put air into it. I tried going less than 50 miles an hour to conserve fuel. The tidewater country then was different than it is now. There were no strip malls and there were still filling stations where they would fix a flat for a few dollars while you waited. I hugged the back roads looking for a cheap place to get the tire fixed.

There were old shacks pressed up against one another, farm stands, small towns where the billboards of movie theaters stuck out over the storefronts. When I couldn't drive any longer, I'd pull the car off the side of the road and try to get some sleep.

In the morning, I was into Delaware and it felt as if the military

Part III—Nothing for Nothing

were really behind me somewhere back in the rearview mirror. It took me a good 20 hours to drive the 450 miles home. Normally, it would have been a seven-hour trip, but I stopped in Scranton to try and sell my camera—a nice Canon I'd bought overseas. No one would give me cash. And I wasted a couple of hours there. In Binghamton, I found a pawn shop and the owner gave me a twenty-dollar bill. The camera was worth a lot more, but I was desperate.

I'd been AWOL again for almost two days and even though I was hungry and worried about money, it felt good to be on my own away from the mindset of the Marine Corps and the spit and polish of Sea School, Marine Barracks, Portsmouth, Virginia. For the first time in two years, I felt as if I was free.

I was 19, three months back from Vietnam and two months' duty at a naval weapons station near Charleston, South Carolina, and it was the first time I had ever done anything to break the rules.

I know, I know I'm repeating things, but that fact still echoes, like someone yelling in a cave. I want to show him the photo of me from Chu Lai when I was still 18—so he can see how young I was, how naïve and just plain ignorant. Now I know, thanks to therapy and good sense, that turning away from the Marines was the first time I began to think for myself—the brainwash and bullshit they'd fed us seemed to gradually fall away, and I could see clearly now the mistake I'd made, the stupidity of my 17-year-old decision to enlist.

The first thing I did in Binghamton after selling my camera was to eat at the cheapest drive-thru burger place I could find—four burgers for one dollar. I hadn't eaten in two days.

Then I drove home and lied to my parents and told them I'd been given another week's leave. They had no reason not to believe me. I'd only been home a short time after my tour of duty in Vietnam, and then I went straight down to the weapons station in Charleston. And I think they didn't mind me coming back home again.

I'd been doing the long weekend ride to see my girlfriend Marie. At the weapons station you got a 96-hour pass every other weekend and a lot of us went north on a *swoop*. You could leave Friday morning after your guard shift was over, and if you had a good car, it was easy to make it north for the weekend.

19. Four Days Gone

It was near the second week in October when I left home again. I pretended I was going back, and my father gave me five bucks for gas. I spent that first night in the front seat of my car on the campus of SUNY Binghamton. Campus security woke me up around 4 a.m. and told me to get off the campus. There was a thin dust of snow on the windshield and the car was cold.

And then I want to explain to Nate about the consequences; turning away came with its costs—jail and military brigs and then a locked hospital psychiatric ward where the violence I had witnessed overseas was mirrored in the men on the ward, men who slashed their wrists, overdosed on pills, or tried to hurt themselves in other ways. And seeing my youngest son sitting across from me, I cannot help but remember how young we all were then, too young to know about how the choices we had made would stay with us, festering and malignant.

And yet, I don't tell him this truth—I try to shrug it off, faking a hardness I never had, a distance that was never there. I keep trying to tell him how it is impossible for me to forget what happened and how it all keeps twisting and turning into what has become my life. He has his own way of seeing now—and it's a good way—he knows he is okay in his own skin, and it gives him a confidence I have never had. I like his attitude and his surety, his ability to face an uncertain future with determination.

For a few minutes after we're home, I watch Nate walk up the gravel driveway, and I sit in the front seat thinking that I wish I could have told my own father what I've told Nate. I wish I might have explained to my father why I ran away, how it had nothing to do with fear. Instead, it was as if I had begun to wake up—and it felt as if a damp fog had lifted, and I could see where I'd been and what had happened. Maybe when my father got older—in his late 70s, he might have understood—he might have seen things from my point of view. I might have been able to tell him how it took me a good while to understand *"We have to unlearn much that we were taught."*

~ ~ ~

20

Running on Empty

No one wants to know about what I did during those days I was running—how I got by, what I did for money, where I slept. It's not that interesting. And now even the guys who gave me a place to stay for a week are gone. I never told any of my sons about what I did during those months I was AWOL. I didn't think they would understand how it was to be without a paycheck, without income, with just my old car and whatever dollars I had scrounged. And no cellphone, no one to call, no way to make contact except by pay phone or in person.

After going up to Albany to visit my friend Bob from high school who was in his junior year of college and crash at his apartment for a week; after writing papers for Bob and Terry, his friend, who were both finance majors and struggling to write essays for their English classes; after realizing that Bob and his friends at Albany were not keen on my AWOL status, and maybe they were not too sure about why I had left the Marine Corps or about what was really going on over there in Vietnam; after I started to understand this, I realized they didn't get my predicament—no incoming cash, except for what I had gotten from my father and the few dollars I had saved up from selling stuff at hock shops—and in fact, a few of the guys who shared an apartment with Terry suggested that maybe I should turn myself in; and it was then I knew I had to leave, had to find some way to keep on.

It was difficult to do this with no place else to go. I knew had to find a job and a place to live, and the winter was starting to come on in upstate New York. Driving back on Route 20, the cold air pressing in around the car, the dull gray of the countryside sliding quickly

20. Running on Empty

into early winter, I felt more alone than ever, and I had to find a way to make some money—a way to keep letting my parents believe I was still in the Marines, only now in Virginia—so it was easier to get home on the weekends to see my girlfriend, who was a high school senior and the sister of my good friend.

I drove back to Binghamton and found a room in a cheap hotel downtown—a place that rented rooms by the week and cost only $10.50 including bed linens. The hotel smelled like rubber when I climbed the wooden staircase to my second-floor room.

Maybe it was just the warm stale air that greeted me as I pushed up the stairs, or the worn staircase itself. The odor seemed like elastic—a kind of burning, rubbery smell. It reminded me of the burning shit detail we had to do in Chu Lai, pulling the cut-in-half 50-gallon drums from beneath the latrines, pouring kerosene on the drums of waste and setting them on fire. The smoke would lift over the battalion HQ and sometimes no one would even look up at the black smoke, the air filled with the stinging smell of burning excrement.

In that downtown rooms-for-rent place, I remember reading myself to sleep, smoking menthol cigarettes. It was the kind of place you didn't want to spend too much time in, so I came back there only to sleep. It was located next to a bunch of used clothing stores and swap shops and you could park in the lot next door for free. And I began to look for work.

The first job I found was making signs in a Giant discount store. The boss was a thin, clean-cut guy and he liked me because I was a high-school graduate and I had an aptitude for words—I could spell. He offered me a job as the sign maker—and stock boy when they needed me—but mostly I made signs for sale items on a machine in the back room. It was part-time and it took me almost two weeks before I got my first paycheck—and by then I was in trouble and really needed the cash, but it was a job.

One afternoon at the Giant my father came in and I had to go back into the sign-making room so he wouldn't see me. Later that same week, Ernie, who worked as a stocker and all-around helper, asked me to have a beer and some food with him after our shift. I agreed and we went to a burger place near the store. When he asked

Part III—Nothing for Nothing

me where I was from, what I was doing about the draft, I told him the truth, figuring I could use a new friend, someone I could confide in, someone to talk to about what I was doing, where I might go next.

I was wrong. The next day when I showed up for work, the boss said he had to let me go—if I were AWOL from the military, he couldn't have me in the store. Ernie had ratted me out so he could take my job as sign maker—a 15-cent-per-hour raise.

I got a job as bun man at a famous burger place and what was great about the work—also only 20 hours a week—was that we got to eat a cheeseburger and fries and other things that were left over from our shift. And now at least I had something to eat every day for free. With the holidays coming, I took a second job in the Trim a Tree department in a supermarket chain with a discount store attached. I also worked as a bagger during heavy shopping times, and I carried items for shoppers to their cars. I was making money now—nearly 60 dollars a week—so between the two jobs, I had some cash. When the manager of the burger chain job said he liked my work and wanted to send me to "school" for training in hamburgerology so I might eventually become an assistant manager, I knew I had to quit.

One day I just didn't show up for my shift and instead took the overtime they had offered me at the supermarket. It was getting cold now, my car's battery died and I had to replace it, and the car needed snow tires. What I remember is carrying bags of plastic trees to cars, the store loudspeakers curling their holiday carols around me. Each trip to the parking lot seemed like a rollercoaster ride through a winding tunnel. I answered an ad in the local paper and found another place to live in a boardinghouse run by a kind and grandfatherly man named Lou Baccatti. You had to pay by the week and share a bathroom down the hall, but there was only one other boarder, the place was clean and well-kept, and I felt safe there. Sometimes when my shift ended at 9 p.m. I would come back to his house, less than a mile from where I worked, and Lou would offer me a cup of coffee downstairs.

That weekend when I came home on Saturday, after my shift was done, I think my father knew something was up—maybe my hair had started to grow out or maybe he could just tell I was not okay. When

20. Running on Empty

I left on Sunday afternoon, pretending to be driving to Virginia, he gave me a book to read—*"You'll probably like this book,"* he said. It was *On the Road* by Jack Kerouac. I don't think my father had read the novel, but in his own way he knew it was a book about driving, and in a literal way—he saw my frantic, fake driving as a statement about who I was, what I had become. In many ways, he was right.

~ ~ ~

21

When You Awake

    Winter came early in 1967. I was still winging it, working the double shifts and eating late—bad food: fried chicken, sandwiches. Still smoking. My fake coming and going was working, and only my girlfriend Marie knew and no one else. One Saturday, she asked me to come to the fall dance at a recreation center. I wore my uniform. Big mistake. Those high school juniors and seniors kept asking me the same question, "How many ----- did you kill?" And I didn't answer.

    Marie was going into the second term of her senior year of high school—she was two years younger than I was—but there was a wide gap between us, growing wider because she just didn't understand what I was doing. I'm not sure there was any way to explain it to her. What had happened, why I was AWOL. Some weekends, I just worked both Saturday and Sunday, and if it were possible maybe I'd drive down to see Marie on Saturday night. And when my parents asked me if I would be home for Christmas, I told them yes.

    The letter from the local chief of police came about two days before Christmas. It was addressed to my father. When he opened it, I knew my running had ended. I now was an officially listed "deserter" from the Marines. And a day after Christmas, I said goodbye to Marie and her parents at their home. I was in uniform. Then my father and I went to Bayliff's Bar on Main Street in Union about a mile from our home. And for the first and only time my father and I had a beer together at the bar, and he asked me a few questions about why I'd gone AWOL, and what I wanted him to do with my car.

    A few weeks later, I got a letter from my father after I'd been transferred to the Brooklyn Brig from the Onondaga County Jail up in Syracuse. I still have his letter. He wrote: *I parked your car up on*

21. When You Awake

some blocks in the back yard. I don't know why you make things so hard for yourself, Gerry. Your Uncle Frank, who was in the Marines at Tarawa, said, "If he's in the brig, he's now an official Marine."

Uncle Frank was the one uncle I had never met, but I guess my father felt better after he called him and they talked. Today, no one really listens when I tell my sons about the brig, about what it was like there—how the staff sergeant made every man who smoked buy a carton of Old Gold cigarettes so he could get himself a new TV with the coupons. So, I smoked Old Golds in the brig, and the first day when we were still getting set up, there was a confrontation between the staff sergeant and one of the guards when the guard told me to take the campaign ribbons off my uniform.

"You be a shitbird, brig rat corporal, so take off those ribbons!"

The sarge came up to the brig guard and pulled him up short.

"Hold it right there. He's been overseas and he gets to wear those ribbons when he's in his uniform, he earned them fuck-for-brains! Where you been? Huh? Stand down!"

And the sergeant made me put the ribbons back on until we were issued our brig utilities.

After a few days, they sent me to St. Albans for a medical exam. The hospital was filled with guys who had been wounded in Vietnam, guys in wheelchairs sitting in the hallways, waiting. I saw some of them look at me when I passed by under escort. The brig doctor asked me why I'd gone AWOL, and when I said I see things, he put me on a tranquilizer called Stelazine. Weeks later I found out this prescription needed an additional pill to go with it or you had the "ants in your pants" feeling. I had never taken any kind of tranquilizer before. The trip to St. Albans Hospital seemed even stranger than it was—the cold January day, the snow outside the windows, the waiting room, the tests. It was good to get back to the open room of the brig where the light came in and you could see the buildings in the distance.

~ ~ ~

22

New Beginnings

Today I'm telling Dr. Morley about how I get lost in corridors. I'm telling him about how I can't find his office in the hall because I start to space out in places like that. I get lost. I know this is hard to understand. I've been seeing the doctor for over three years, and I still get confused when I walk through the glass doors, so I wait for him to come out, to come and get me. My wife, Michele, does not understand. She laughs at me. It happens often, this sense of displacement, of being in a familiar place and having it seem unfamiliar. Hallways, corridors, underground parking lots, especially those with few people.

~ ~ ~

PART IV

In the Zone

23

I Walk the Line

At Sea School, Marine Barracks in Norfolk, Virginia, they sent me to the Portsmouth Brig. It must have been the MP sergeant's recommendation that did it. *"He said he sees things,"* the sarge wrote in his report. I had to run all the way in with my seabag overhead and the brig guards screaming at me to move faster.

"Move out, move out," the guards kept shouting.

I stumbled into the bunk area and the other prisoners there looked up at me.

"Do you know where the fuck you are, shit head?"

"Virginia, sir," I said.

The sergeant of the unit looked at me.

"Asshole," he said. *"You see that line there running down the deck?"*

"Yes sir," I said.

"Well, asshole, that's my line. You step over it or on it and I fuck you up."

I never made it to dinner that night. The 1st sergeant in charge of the brig interviewed me that afternoon, and I couldn't sit still.

"What's the matter with you?" he asked. *"You got ants in your pants?"*

"No sir," I said.

I didn't tell him that the doc in the Brooklyn Brig had put me on some tranquilizers. Stelazine. He could have read it in my papers, but who knows what he'd read or hadn't read.

"What kinds of things you see?"

I couldn't tell him about the dreams, about the wounded, about the children at the dump screaming. Instead, I told him I saw a rabbit, a big rabbit.

23. I Walk the Line

The 1st sergeant smiled. *"A bunny rabbit? What the ... you seen that movie,* Harvey?"

"No sir." I didn't know what he was talking about.

"You know, it's about a guy who talks to a rabbit."

"No, sir."

"You got to go to seclusion, solitary cell. We can't have no crazy fucks on the open yards."

I spent the next four days and nights in a cell. They passed my meals in on a tray. I read the Bible and wondered what would happen next. I thought about the letter I got from my father while I was in the brig in Brooklyn. He said he didn't understand why I'd gone AWOL after the war was over for me. *"Why now?"* he wanted to know. He said to keep my chin up, that they'd keep my car up on blocks until I got home.

The sergeant who had come up from Virginia to take me back was a good guy, and he'd been overseas. He was also Italian American.

On the plane, after we had our seats, he said he would take the handcuffs off.

"It's just you and me. No reason to make a run for it now. Where were you over there?"

~ ~ ~

Out of a dream the dull thudding as if someone were pounding on a wooden door. At first quietly but gaining, growing louder. And then suddenly awake, I heard the shouts of the others, the sound growing closer.

"Hey," Ota whispered across at me. "Wake up, wake up, man."

"I'm awake," I said in the darkened tent.

Mortars. The word caught me up, and pushing the wool blanket off I grabbed what gear I could. We hadn't been issued rifles yet.

"Move out, move out." The voice gruff.

And then the thump, the explosions. They were nearer now.

"They've hit the HQ depot," Ota said. I could see his glasses reflecting the dull glow.

"Let's go. Let's go."

Outside, the company area was filled with men. I fell over some

Part IV—In the Zone

wooden pallets, and Ota picked me up, pushed me into the sandbagged bunker.

"Get down," he said.

Then the dull thudding stopped. Out along the ridgeline on the highway, a truck's headlights flared. A crush of voices from the other bunkers. I shivered in the early morning chill. The breeze off the ocean smelled of fish and diesel oil.

"Smoke?" Ota asked, then pushed the cigarette pack at me, cupping the light. "Relax," he said, "it's over for now."

My first week in country. But I was lucky. By then Griggs was already dead—he stepped on a mine his first day out. Griggs, sitting on a barstool in Okinawa, smiling at the barmaid. He'd spent all his money. "He knew he wouldn't make it," Madlock said. Griggs, Brent I. His name rubbed on a wall of names. July 20, 1966.

~ ~ ~

After the doctor's evaluation at the medical center adjacent to the Portsmouth Brig, I was sent back to the commanding officer of Sea School, Marine Barracks. In a brief meeting—the major asked me to relax and stand easy—he told me they were going to send me to the hospital for an evaluation.

"Corporal," he said, clearing his throat and staring at me. I was still standing at attention. And anxious, moving a little back and forth—a reaction from the tranquilizer they'd given me in Brooklyn without the additive—so that it felt as if I had ants in my pants and an itchy all over feeling I couldn't shake.

"Corporal, I admit I don't know what's wrong with you, but they'll figure it out, I guess." He looked at me over the top of his glasses, "I confess I don't have a goddamn clue."

I didn't say anything.

"Sergeant," he told the 1st sergeant who had escorted me into his office. "Get the corporal an escort to the hospital."

The two guys who had the job of taking me to the hospital had heard about the rabbit. So, they started to crack up as soon as they'd gotten me into the back seat of the pickup. "A little bunny rabbit huh?"

23. I Walk the Line

"How fucking' crazy is that?"

"Are you crazy, corporal? Are you loony tunes? Well, that's where we're takin' you to—the loony bin—Ward 13." They kept slapping each other, laughing.

The thin guy who wasn't driving was having a good time. "What's this bunny look like? Huh?"

They were clueless—in fact, instead of escorting me inside the hospital, they dropped me at the front walkway and let me walk in by myself. Not too smart since they were responsible for my check-in. I could have walked right out after they'd pulled away, but I didn't.

I'd come this far, I told myself. Might as well take it through and see what happens. Now, what I'm remembering is the day—how warm it was for January, the sun shining and the air fresh and cool. I hadn't been outside since they put me in solitary at the brig. So, it felt good to walk into the hospital, like it was the start of something new. And it was good to be out of the lockup. I'd been in jails or brigs for over a month.

~ ~ ~

24

I Got Dreams to Remember

Listen, Bo. Wake up! They take the first three dreams you have and call them memory. You never dream anything else.

"Remember when they pulled out your first tooth, hey? Do you remember that?"

I looked at him. "Yeah. I remember. Pliers. The guy had, like, pliers and he pulls it out with a twist. You feel it give—thwock—just like that the socket gives way. I know."

"Well, that is what he let them do, man," Perry said. "He let them take out all his f--- teeth."

"Why?"

"Hey, that's what I wanna know," Perry said.

It was getting dark, and they'd be pushing the tractor carts in, getting us ready for the sleep zone.

"I'm short," Perry said. *"What do I care?"*

Outside we could sense the spring coming, we could see the light lingering at the windows, we could smell the air. It had a scent of blossoms in it, blossoms smiling in on us, eh? A sweetness lingering.

But time has a way of fooling us; days seemed to suspend and stretch out like weeks. Maybe it was the anti-depressants, the tranquilizers—bombers—administered every four to six hours by our friendly corpsmen to keep us cool. Maybe time was ours—keeping us safe from the events of the world—safe and warm like caterpillars in our cocoons. It was easy to make friends there—and easy too to know who was well enough to be a friend and which ones were the deep-enders, the guys who would be shipping out for other hospitals, special units closer to home.

24. I Got Dreams to Remember

We watched them go one Friday after I first got in. Perry and I sat on the chairs near the nurse's station and watched them strap down three or four men on stretchers. Perry said it was the night flight to Philly—Philadelphia being the big house—the waystation for the serious freaks. From there you went to the VA hospital that was closest to your hometown. We all thought we were getting tickets for Philly when we first checked in.

That's where they send you if you're in the Navy or the Marines, you got to go to Philly. If you're in the Army, you go south to Walter Reed. We looked over at the four who were leaving us.

"Zombs," Perry said. *"You know, deep-enders."*

Outside the light was fading and night came on. We got nervous in the dusk, anxious as the shadows deepened. Perry had a full cast on his lower right leg—he said he broke it jumping ship, but Frenchy said it was part of Perry's problem, the reason he was getting out. He tried to take himself out, Frenchy had said. You know, fake or real, it makes no difference. They got to believe you. Frenchy was cool. We'd smoke menthols together and he'd tell stories of his trips. He'd been in the Navy for a couple years, done some traveling. He was smart too; he always wanted to know what it was I was reading, what I did before. And I was kind of a celeb for a while. The day they brought me in I was still in those dress greens, fresh from the brig. And there were a lot of stares until the doc interviewed me and they suited me up in blue PJs and robe. And Frenchy had been the first one to come over and tell me the next morning:

"Hey, man," he'd said. *"You know you can get out from here?"*

I told him I didn't know that. I was just trying to get out of the brig. He smiled then and said it again as if he were not sure he believed me.

"You can get out of the service from here."

I watched him walk back to his bunk as the doctor and the corpsmen came through for morning call. He was short, skinny, suntanned, with black curly hair. He had that sincere way of making you believe he had the scoop on everyone. Later Perry and I found out that Frenchy had turned in 10 or 15 guys on his boat for drugs in order to get out of his own set of drug charges—he'd narced 'em out.

Part IV—In the Zone

And then he tried to kill himself. He had to do something. The rest of the boat was after him. So, he tried to slash his wrists. It did the trick and that's how he got here.

We all had our ways in. Getting out was a bit different, but getting in was easy enough. That's what I mean about time. Inside the ward time seemed to drift and stand still. As if we were in the horse latitudes, as if the ward was a big ship floating without a breeze, caught in the still cold of winter. Frenchy was the first friend I made there. He was good enough to get to go to OT, and he was smart enough to know that if you got to go to OT, you got off the ward for an hour or so and that was good. Any way to get off the ward was good, because the hours dragged. There was only an old black-and-white TV that got a couple of channels, a Ping-Pong table, a few card tables and some board games. The books were old spy novels and *Reader's Digests*, comic books if someone had left a few behind—Superman and Captain Marvel.

~ ~ ~

25

If You Want Me to Stay

In the hospital-issue dark blue robe and light blue tie-string pajamas I thought of my stepmother and how she defined me in red—dressed me in red and my brother in blue. When I first got free of her, I wore only blue for years—light blue chambray work shirts and denim shirts or dark blue sweaters—cardigans and pullovers. Today I have one red sweater. Perhaps for my stepmother, color was a way of defining what we could and could not do. I envied my brother for his blue. Blue to me then and now is a color full of possibility—the sky, a lake, a coolness. Blue was what I could not have and because it was kept from me, because I was not allowed to wear it, and because it suggested possibilities, it was a color I wanted, a color that seemed to agree with the part of me that wanted to escape. As for my brother, perhaps he too wanted those red shirts, the red colors. The dusk and dawn of things. For me, red was anger, disappointment, grief. Red was the bad marks in school; the color of shame and regret. I don't think my stepmother knew how color would shape and define us. I don't think she realized that her insistence on colors, on dressing us in similar outfits, in forcing a pattern on us, would have a different set of consequences as we got older.

If color were one way my stepmother had of separating us, of distinguishing us, there were other things she did to let us learn what she expected of us as boys. As the oldest, I earned the right to get the first tryouts in what she felt boys should do. The first of these trials was my Little League baseball career. It went like this. I was not what they call "a natural." I was not coordinated. I couldn't run very fast. In fourth grade I'd been given a pair of glasses when they realized I couldn't see the blackboard. I was nearsighted, too. My stepmother

Part IV—In the Zone

and my father drove me to the ball field where the tryouts were being held. My father, who had never played a team sport in his life besides street stickball while he was growing up in Hell's Kitchen, spoke to the coach. First mistake.

The coach was a six-foot-three, gangly sort of cross between John Wayne and Gary Cooper without any screen presence. His son was the pitcher and his nephew played first base. The coach, whose last name was Morris, had a close crewcut with enough goop in it to keep his hair standing up even in the worst rainstorm. He hated non-athletic, bookworm types, which he decided I was from the moment he spied me staring out from behind my father. He was witty and cruel. But smart enough to know he had to give me a shot to keep the league "open" and so he made me the second baseman. During our first game, I surprised myself, the coach and his son by catching a hard-hit line drive. *"Beginner's luck,"* the shortstop muttered when I stood there dazed, the ball stuck in my mitt. My first time at bat, the pitcher from the opposing team tagged me on the shoulder with the ball and I got a walk. After that first game, I never really got to practice with the team.

The coach told me the wrong day to show up, or he gave me the wrong field. When my stepmother got the coach on the telephone to ask if it were deliberate, he shrugged it off. *"You must've got the wrong field; you must've missed us."* That day my stepmother drove me to practice, and they let me take a couple of strikeouts and catch a few fly balls. When practice was over, the coach told me to come back to the same field the next day at the same time. When I showed up the next day with my new mitt and uniform, there was a game being played, but it was by the local bar team and it was a softball game. The Little League was not there.

After that I got the drift, and I told my stepmother that I didn't want to play baseball anymore. A fight ensued. Shouts, her angry insistence that a boy should play baseball, that otherwise I'd end up a sissy. All my years in junior high school and high school, my stepmother recounted this early failure of mine. She would tell relatives, friends or perfect strangers about the time I tried out for Little League, and she would always end it with how they hadn't wanted me to play.

25. If You Want Me to Stay

Years later, when I was in graduate school in the Midwest, I met the coach's son again. He was a bartender at one of the university watering holes, he had flunked out of undergrad, and he hadn't played baseball in years. He didn't remember me from the team.

~ ~ ~

26

There's a Hole in the Future

After the testing was over, the doctors treated me as a specimen in a round table—meaning the whole NPS crew was present, including the doctor who had conducted the testing on me. I was escorted into a conference room where the doctors waited in a circle of chairs—each one in his or her lab coat. I got a seat near the door, a bit forward of the circle. Dr. Spencer was the head of the unit and he was my doctor; he did the intake on me when I'd first come over from the brig.

"Tell us about the war. What you remember." His question stopped the muttering, the shuffle of papers.

I busied myself with playing with the button on my robe. I lit a cigarette. *"Yes,"* I said. *"I remember it. It's not something I want to forget."* He nodded, a little surprised, and I could see him tuck his head into the lab coat—turtle-like, a small gesture of satisfaction. There is a hand that goes up from one of the new, younger doctors.

"But you went AWOL," he says.

"Yes." I tell him. *"I did...."*

"Does it still bother you?" he asks.

I catch his eyes—and stare. *"Yup."*

Dr. Spencer changes the subject, asks me to talk about the waking, about the rabbit.

Then another doctor asks me about girls.

"Do you like girls?" he asks.

"Yes, I like girls, I had a girlfriend before I went AWOL, before I turned myself in."

"When do you see this rabbit?" Dr. Spencer asks.

26. There's a Hole in the Future

"*Do you see other things?*" the older doc who tested me asks.

I don't tell them about the ghosts. *"No,"* I say. *"Only the rabbit."*

"*He's big?*" another one asks.

"Yes, five feet tall at least."

It goes on like this. I don't know what I'm doing. Is it a test? Have I passed? Why are all these doctors interviewing me? Do they believe me? What will happen if they don't?

"*I know things like this don't exist,*" I tell them. Dr. Spencer smiles.

~ ~ ~

I let my mind drift back to them again. I have recognized their presence for so long—the crows circling my car in the early morning on a back road, the curious old man who stopped me in the street to ask directions, the presence I felt behind me on the stairs. All of these signs I had refused to see, what I had turned away from. One night the ghosts of TK and Jip came and sat near my bed. It was Jack who spoke first—dragging on his cigarette, clearing his throat in the West Virginia drawl. Or I imagined he spoke. Maybe his words just floated through time—back across the years as if over a wire—vibrating as if the wind had made the wire move and not time and distance and the slip of memory. And I saw the trucks again. I forgot the doctors looking at me in their semicircle of chairs, I forgot the major shaking his head behind his desk, I forgot the hospital ward and the stuffy, closed-in feeling of the open ward. I watched the convoy coming down the white road, and I felt the sweat begin on the back of my neck.

~ ~ ~

27

Goin' Out of My Head

Dingbat Lee loved Little Anthony & the Imperials as much as any of us. He also liked to dry banana peels on the radiators because he believed (or someone told him) you could get high smoking dried banana peels. But the ward corpsman, TJ, caught him with those peels and it was all up.

Dingbat was tall, over six feet, and big, like over two hundred pounds. He had a shock of black hair that had been trimmed close, and he used to brush it down over his forehead. He was the greatest Ping-Pong player anyone had ever seen—including the doctors and nurses and corpsmen on the ward. He'd play two people at the same time—and laugh at how inept they were. No one could come close to beating Dingbat Lee in Ping-Pong. It was his game. And he liked the "dingbat" tag Perry had given him; in fact, he kind of started to use it himself—he'd introduce himself like that, you know, to those new guys coming in. He'd say, *"Hey, pleased to meet you, I'm Dingbat Lee."*

But then they caught him trying to get it on with his wife in the ward office visiting room and things changed. Dingbat refused meds at night. He refused to cooperate in ward cleanups. He'd sit around and watch TV and you knew he was planning something. And it wasn't too long before we found out what it was. Late one night after meds, after the lights were dimmed and the shift had changed, Dingbat Lee and Perry (who had a cast on one leg up to his knee) decided to toss the big TV into the ward office window. Luckily the window was reinforced with wire—but it did break—and then everything got quickly out of hand.

They called it a riot, but it wasn't really a riot, only the two of them causing a major disturbance, except on Ward 13, there were

27. Goin' Out of My Head

some serious crazies—and those guys joined in as the lights started to flicker on and the alarm sounded. One dude started to beat a tune on his metal nightstand that was bolted to the wall. Another guy just started to scream as loud as he could. And it all quickly grew into a pandemonium.

That was how Lee and Perry ended up in the quiet rooms or QRs as we called the two padded cell-like rooms at the end of the ward. They strapped them down and hit them both with shots of Thorazine. And that was the end of the TV, the end of Lee's Ping-Pong tournaments too, since the table was trashed. Now we had no TV and no Ping-Pong table and I'm glad I'm getting close to a release date, close to whatever it was that waited for me outside, at home.

~ ~ ~

28

Song of the Wind

Listen, let me find another starting point, a place to let you into things so you can see what I saw. K? To connect the me from now with the me from then. I like to think we both exist simultaneously, that we have passed each other in the hall, maybe even nodded a greeting once or twice. Dangerous to believe in a dual reality, to believe that these two selves exist at the same time, that all the while I've been sleepwalking, my other self has been doing his thing on the outside. And that's the rip you see, alone or together we've been doing the same thing—escaping, turning away, call it what you will. The result has been the same. And my wake up has paralleled his wake up. This is one reason why it is difficult for me to remember things in order, precisely the way they occurred. Whenever I look back on the time before the sleep, what comes back are glimpses of who I was then, the kind of man I had become—or perhaps even further back to the boy I was, to my childhood. Crib years?

Each time it seems as if I am crawling on a long runway and planes are taking off all around me. I don't hear the noise of the engines, but I feel the awful vibration as if the wings were flapping, as if they were giant birds—prehistoric rocs that swooped up and away from me.

I started to imagine I was the "long walker" or "the deep six." I started to believe I would be trapped here. And suddenly, I saw myself cruising the locked ward and picking up things: watches, photos, packs of cigarettes and gum. I guess it caused a bit of disturbance on the ward. And so they tagged me. A deep six. I wasn't supposed to wake up. They had me figured for a permanent zone, or at least that's what the call was back then.

28. Song of the Wind

Now, I know it was just my own myopia, my own paranoid brain thinking I would be trapped in an NPS ward or sent to some other hospital and I started to flip.

I began to doubt my own sanity. I bought the craziness. I was hooked. And for a while I was lost.

Now that I am awake, I have begun to piece together how I came here, and as the doctor says, what kept me here, asleep, the king of sleepwalkers. Once you've been a sleepwalker, it's easy to recognize the other people who are in the same state.

I used to see them in the hospital—nurses, doctors, corpsmen, visitors who've come to pay their respects. No, not to me. I didn't get visitors. But I recognize the look, you see, the glazed eyes, the inability to see the pain that others feel, a deliberate looking away as if by avoiding the truth one might escape it. Yes? I call the look on these faces the drone look. And since I've woken up, I have made a resolution to keep on waking up, to push each day out and try to recapture some of that lost time. Impossible, I know. But when I look back it seems the past was one long black tunnel, dark and tilted sideways, and I keep trying to right it, to bring the ship to rest, to get the kelson—the internal keel—to make it right.

Don't get me wrong, the ghosts are still there. Now I've come to recognize some of them and I know enough to keep them to myself. We all have our ghosts, I suppose. These are the pictures I drew when I first came here—swirls of color, lines and always the presence of enormous dark wings fluttering overhead, suffocating me with a sweetness and tremendous surges of breath.

~ ~ ~

But now I know that those two selves—the one from then and the other me from now—met up once or twice. I mean their paths crossed—they passed each other. I used to imagine that there was a man at a bar who was drinking quietly, and as I watched him, he would turn toward me without knowing me. He was alone, mysterious because I had not seen him in the place before, and I knew the clientele well. I knew the faces of the people who drank there. Yet he seemed familiar, as if we knew each other from someplace else, as if we had

Part IV—In the Zone

met at a party or a social event. And I felt this man—older than most of the young people there—was somehow connected to me, to who I would become. It was as if I were him in some future time. Years later, going back to the bar on a crowded weekday evening, I sat alone on a stool and stared at myself in the mirror behind the rows of bottles, wondering if it had happened, if I had become that other man.

~ ~ ~

The first flowers, those morning glories of heavenly blue and the moonflowers, reminded me of the other flowers, giant white ones with petals as big as a man's hand, the blossoms so magnificent one had to blink to make sure they were real because the heat, so intense and glaring, made it difficult to believe what one saw. The jungle canopy and the waves of trees, ringed with blossoms, and beyond those the stark gray cliffs and the open water of the sea—a blue so dark, almost purple against the shimmering trees.

And then of course the sound too, the noise of the jets coming in low onto the metal landing strips, a makeshift runway until the heavy equipment could move in to pave up the sand, the trucks and heavy-duty forklifts. It took a little time to know where I was, to realize the necessities waiting behind the illusion, to see the flowers explode. I don't remember the war very well; it is not that I have forgotten it, but I don't remember things in a straight line. I start with one day and go on to the next and then the time seems jumbled, mixed-up; the whole scene like a cutting floor, the film jammed and different frames pieced together with other ones so that the consistency is wrong, there's no coherence.

One night the ghosts of Marty and Jenkins came and sat near my bed. There they both were, sitting together, smoking cigarettes. I never told about the ghosts or the nightmares. I learned that much, keep your dreams to yourself.

And so here they were, sitting together and looking at me. And it was Jenkins who spoke first, clearing his throat and drawling in that East Tennessee way he had. "Whail, you been avoidin' it, LT, that's what Marty here says." Now I says to him that I left before any of it happened, you know.

28. Song of the Wind

They don't need to speak, but Marty turns his head a bit and I can see there's only half of his face left. Jenkins is still whole, or looks it, gangly, toothless and older. And then I know they want me to follow them back there to where the canopy opens and the sound comes back in a roar.

They got nervous when I told people I could see auras around them. The funny short corpsman who shared his smokes with me when I first got there, I remember the look he gave me when I told him I could sense things. I could see his eyes, see the glow he gave off.

You know, folks didn't go for that kind of talk. They thought I was really going for things, pushing the limits so to speak. So, I didn't let on I had the view. It's not something new anyway. I mean, it's not something I developed there in the wards. It was not something to do with my condition. I'd had it for a long time. But, I didn't recognize it; that's it, you see, to understand that sometimes one's own intuition—one's own gut feeling about things is all there is. So, I call it the aura now, the way I have of telling whether or not a person is telling the truth, whether or not a person is at his or her best—truthful. Because there are a lot of people who believe the things they say, who are convinced of the things they go on about. This won't work with them; it's the others, the deliberate untruths you might say, the real truth stretchers, eh? And as I began to reach around me, to see where I was, to understand how I'd come here, I began to think that there was a hidden language to the flowers I wanted to plant. I began to understand that I needed to nurture the flowers in the yard as much as I needed to face the truths about myself—how I came here and how, possibly, I might leave.

~ ~ ~

"LT, the voice says, tugging, hey LT, you there man?"

And I turn around to see PK grinning at me.

"Where you been LT? We been lookin' for you."

The smoke clears, the candles lit at different tables inside the tent. In the haze I can see PK, and Jack, and Puff, MD, staring back at me. And the film starts again. I'm talking to them, but it seems as if I am someone else, that someone else is playing my part.

Part IV—In the Zone

"OK, let's take that ride," I hear myself say. The night is dark and hot and there is only a breath of cool air just starting to come out of the mountains behind the camp.

Puff murmurs that he'll do the driving and jumps into the cab of the PC.

PK and Ward climb in back.

"Leave the flaps open," I tell them, "so you can see what's going on."

Puff starts the motor, and we ease out of the compound toward the gate.

The sentry waves us through and we move out onto the dirt road and then the tarmac of the highway. Now all of it—the blackness of the night, the road without lights, the small villages pressed up against the road, the smoke of cooking fires and the fish smells and stale rotting smells of cooking and refuse, a vegetable dark that encircles us so that across from me in the cab Puff's face is a dark glow in the dash lights, so dark now that the night seems to surround us, envelop us in a thick curtain. We are lost, I think, lost and driving down a narrow road that doesn't lead anywhere but to another group of huts, tin-roofed and darker still beside the road. Headlights pass, a truck convoy heading out toward the mountains and then dark again. A dog on the road ahead caught in the headlights, disappears in the bushes near the narrow bridge. And then the MP checkpoint. The PC slowing, Puff ducking his head into the collar of his shirt, the Black sergeant chevrons glistening, and me sitting up straighter in the seat—flashing the 1st lieutenant's bars at the sentry. Smiling at us both, he cautions, "Be careful, sir, lots of activity tonight."

And then the guard post receding—leaning into the dark again, that thick dark almost like molasses—so sweet and deep that it seems we are driving off into a widening tunnel—and the tunnel engulfs us in its immensity.

~ ~ ~

I shook it off somehow. Maybe it was the medication that caused my flip. But in late March, I started to realize I was just not okay. I was different and whole somehow.

28. Song of the Wind

Now, I check my C files from the VA, and I see this really happened—I got another battalion office hours for being outside the battalion base camp after hours. I'm the only one the sentry reported. The other guys got off. It's there in my military records even though remembering the night it seems like a crazy, dumbass thing to do. Take a couple of guys who were going to "booby trap school" with Corporal Burns, a few beers and they're in the back of the PC and Puff is driving with his borrowed sergeant emblems and me with two silver lieutenant bars next to him. Just plain crazy.

~ ~ ~

29

Catch the Wind

After a week or two of examinations and conferences with Dr. Spencer, I qualified for occupational therapy. This was a new activity and offered an escape from the monotony of the ward. Our group consisted of Perry, Frenchy, Ryan, and a few others; about seven men in all. The sessions were held in a greenhouse; the winter sun in Virginia was warm and sometimes with the screens open, the smell of the harbor and the sea came through and made you think of other places.

The naval medical officer who ran the OT was nice and she always had a project for us to do, usually something with clay that would get painted and fired in a kiln, especially projects that took more than one session. As she explained, she wanted us to use our hands to shape and work the clay. She gave us pages of photos to look at with different designs. I chose a Buddha and a triangle ashtray. They were simple—or so it seemed. And both projects would take some time. Although we didn't know it, by then the Tet Offensive in Vietnam had changed the way Americans and many other people all over the world viewed the war. We didn't get the news on the ward TV—or if we did, no one ever had it on. Usually, the television was tuned to old shows and movies. And we got to walk over to the greenhouse with our corpsmen escorts—in our blue robes and PJs—and for an hour or so it felt as if we were somewhere else. The OT was offered two times a week and was voluntary. For me, it felt as if for the first time in months, I was free.

I knew this was an illusion, but it worked. We got to go over to the greenhouse twice a week, weekdays only. It was strange walking through the regular part of the naval hospital dressed in pajamas

29. Catch the Wind

and our blue robes and slippers. We noticed the stares we got from the "normal" people who were visiting those veterans who were in the open wards, who had been wounded or who were hospitalized with other ailments. Norfolk was a Navy town, and you could tell that from the activity in the hospital.

Ryan decided he wanted to "show off" our craziness after a couple weeks, so one day in OT he "borrowed" some long feathers and the next time we walked over to the greenhouse we pretended to be Native Americans. It was in bad taste for certain, but it gave us a kind of "crazy" solidarity until Willard, one of the Ward 13 corpsmen who escorted us over, said we had to quit the "war whoop" stuff or we wouldn't be allowed to go. As a result, we started to pretend (without feathers) that we were crazier than we really were, and though our escort corpsman frowned on this, he couldn't really prevent us from making weird faces and the like. Finally, the head nurse on the ward got the scoop and spoke to us about it. If we wanted OT, she said we had to stop the bullshit immediately. Ryan got angry and refused to go, so our group was cut down to six.

~ ~ ~

30

My Back Pages

Hey Bo, let me tell you about how crazy it was, pretending I was a spy, a spook without a gun, just a shoulder holster. And how I let the leather straps on the holster show so if you saw it you might think I had a weapon. Empty. Like the long weekends I took to meet Bernadette in some upstate town not far from where she went to college.

Lake towns. Yes. We idealize the past, make it better than it was. Or I do, since I didn't grow up on the wrong side of Baltimore like Turner or in Chicago's Black neighborhood like Ward. Whenever I try to slip into an emotional backwash, daydreaming about growing up in a factory town with a bustling Main Street that boasted two department stores, a Woolworth's with a counter and another five-and-dime with a downstairs bargain basement; whenever I let myself ease into some fake nostalgia, I remember listening to friends talk about what it would be like to leave home, and I feel the pull of nostalgia take place, a wish to make something better than it was, to make it whole and good and decent.

And then I hear those guys chiding me, "Wake up, man—think about who you are and where you came from—are you a Monkees' fan?" And laughing, they get me to start laughing, too. And I know I can't re-invent what was never there in the first place, as much as I want to, and instead I remember sitting in a bus station waiting to catch a ride to meet B. from my duty station in North Carolina—a Marine air base with little to do if you were underage and without a car. Those short homecomings were always fraught with a double reality—of how time seemed split in two by my leaving in the first place, and how I was now a different person, a stranger to myself and to my parents and to my younger brother and even to Bernadette. More

30. My Back Pages

alone than I had ever been before. Now, I imagine how things might have been different if I had stayed home, gone to a community college or taken a job in the factories, instead of enlisting in the Marines at 17 and forcing the issue, waking up with my head shaved and the drill instructors yelling at me to wake up.

I did. In those bus stations with their hard-backed wooden benches, I began to see my country for the first time. And not with shades on, or blinders either. And meeting Turner and Ward six months later, I knew then leaving home in the stupid, abrupt way I had left was a one-way ticket. There was no going back.

Now I'm trying to explain this to myself again, trying to understand what was behind my decision to enlist. Was it a way to escape my parents and their demands?

Was it the feeling of being stranded in my town—no car, no license, no way to get around? I think for a time I believed this, but now I know it was something deeper, more challenging. It was a way to find out who I was—and not as my stepmother believed—that the military would make a man out of me. It did the opposite—the more the military pounded the rules and discipline into me, the groupthink of acting as one team, losing your individuality, the more I realized I had traded one confinement for another, one stupidity for another. And the bad thing about it was there was no way to stop it or change it. I think the hasty enlistment was born in the vague ideas I had about what it meant to be a soldier, what the movies had fed me about glory and duty and the "old lies." Like so many of the young men I came to know in the places I was sent to—Parris Island, Camp Lejeune, Cherry Point, and then Camp Pendleton and Okinawa—until my arrival in Vietnam the summer when I was just six months into being 18, I was idealistic, naïve, ignorant of the very truths that came in like waves, truths I was still unable to recognize.

And smoke fills the room, sweet smoke and dream material filters into the set. You get to seeing how things really were—what the factual stuff lets you forget, you know. Like the underlying truths, the painful double dose of what went down. Like saying yes, when what you really mean is no, no way, no how, no chance. Like what happened after you left, how some guys disappeared—and there was no trace of them on

Part IV—In the Zone

the wall of names or in the old obits of small-town papers. Psychological Ops. You know? Weird shit.

It took some time to lose the idealism, even after coming home—it was like a shadow I couldn't shake, a logjam I couldn't break out of, and things kept piling up and so I turned inward to drugs and drinking, anything to escape and pretend. Avoid personal human contact. Avoid telling people how you feel. Pretend you don't care. Be aloof. Act indifferent, moody, hard to understand. And sooner or later the pretense becomes who you are—like an old field jacket you started wearing to protect you from being just a person and then you can't seem to take it off.

~ ~ ~

31

Ain't Nothing Like the Real Thing

 Glen had only been on the ward for a few days. He'd recently come back from Vietnam and on the train to his new duty station in Virginia, he flipped out. I think he was in the Marines because once he'd been evaluated, they were sending him to the big hospital in Philadelphia. That was usually the place for Marines and Navy—Army guys went to Walter Reed in D.C. I remember Glen because he was younger than I was—he'd just turned 19. And something had happened to him overseas.

 He went crazy inside the train he was on, believing the people in the car with him were all Viet Cong and he was their prisoner. They had to get help to strap him down. He'd hurt others in the passenger car, and when they finally had him subdued and tied down, he was still screaming. They must have called the police. He came into the ward in a straitjacket, and they put him in the QR or quiet room with its padded walls until the shot of Thorazine wore off.

 The next day, I talked to him and I could feel his sadness and sense his disorientation. He knew he was not okay, and he kept saying that over and over. I got him to sit down and play in our endless rummy card game; by the second day, he'd calmed down some—even cracked a smile when Perry made a joke. Glen knew he was going to get the transfer in another day or so, and there were others scheduled to go up "north" as we called the hospital in Philly.

 He didn't want to talk about where he'd been, but he did talk about what had happened on the train, how he just started to hallucinate, and nothing would make it right. He got riled up as he told us about it, and I tried to get him talking about other

Part IV—In the Zone

things—his family, where his home was, what he wanted to do next.

What I remember most is the night he left the ward. There were five or six men who all strapped down on stretchers. They'd been given one of the yellow/orange bombers (sleeping pills) we were forced to take every night. Those pills made you drowsy pretty fast. Wise guys like Perry and Ryan tried not to swallow them when the nurse who doled them out was not paying attention. They thought they'd get higher if they saved a few doses up. Most of the time they made certain you took the pills, but I know Perry got away with not taking it a couple times. Seeing Glen that night in the yellow glow of the ward office with the lights dimmed and the ward growing into its own quiet—it's something I cannot forget. There was a kind of finality to it. And I knelt down next to Glen and talked with him until it was time for the flight, and the corpsmen made us get into our beds.

~ ~ ~

32

New Beginnings

    I'm trying to tell Dr. Morley about how I "turned away" from the Marines, I'm trying to explain how the rabbit story was a "hoax" as Dr. Spencer notes in my medical records, but beneath the hoax was the other stuff—the war stories we carry with us like stones, like a sack of stones. It's what Dr. Morley means by moral guilt—the hard edges of memory and the indifference of time. He knows. I show him the letter written by a psychologist from my undergrad college. He says, *"You don't have to prove to me you have PTSD."*

Part V
Waking Up

33

Slippin' into Darkness

My last homecoming was the real one. There was a finality to it. I'd been discharged. It was eight months later—after being AWOL, listed as a deserter, spending time in Syracuse at the Onondaga County Jail, and then later transferred to the Brooklyn Brig and finally to the Portsmouth/Norfolk Brig in Virginia. I was discharged from the Marines in April, the day they buried Martin Luther King, Jr. I'd spent two months and change on a locked ward of the Neuro Psychiatric Unit in Norfolk Naval Hospital.

The cab driver snorted when I told him I wanted to go to the bus station in downtown Norfolk. *"You ain't going there. Those folks is riotin.' Best bet is the airport."*

~ ~ ~

The cab driver was right—the whole country seemed to be on fire again. There were riots in Norfolk and Newark. My parents picked me up at the airport in Binghamton, the largest of the three towns that made up the Triple Cities. There were no riots there.

But I felt as if I'd brought a weight with me. The new, stiff civilian clothes made me itch. The Marines had forced me to go home without my uniforms; two lance corporals had divided up what I had in my seabag, taking what they wanted. It was illegal to do this, but I didn't care. They claimed it was because I'd been discharged from the hospital. I was bloated from the tranquilizers, from the months inside the locked ward, from the hours with nothing to do. I spent my first few days home driving my old car into northern Pennsylvania, feeling as if I were free of the military at last, unsure of what to do next, where to go.

33. Slippin' into Darkness

I got my first job out of the state employment office—truck driver and stone cutter's apprentice. The pay was good, and I got to drive a flatbed full of flagstone and marble slabs. I liked the stares the workmen gave me at the job sites. I smoked thin cigars and growled at people. I liked the idea of movement, how the truck seemed to rise above the other things. Once I even went to look for Marie in my old fatigue trousers and white T-shirt. I pulled the truck up to her house still loaded for a delivery. She wasn't home, and her mother answered the door and made me talk about the hospital. I left and had three drinks before I went back to work.

I liked the dust rising from behind the flatbed truck—the thin clouds of it blew away toward the east, settling like pollen on the chicory weeds near the entrance to the stone quarry. Chalk dust, stone dust. Old man Mortensen motioning with his hands to slow down. And me easing the rig up into position near the open garage doors.

Tract homes, deliveries of slate for sidewalks, patios, stone walls. White aluminum-sided homes along the bluffs above the river. And the other days Mortensen showed me how to score the stone—chalk line, then chisel. At the end of the day, my hands had swelled from the pounding.

~ ~ ~

There's a river back there, brown and muddy in August heat. A river running alongside the towns where I grew up; its name stays with me wherever I go; its wandering course part of my life. *Susquehanna.* Even today its name brings back my Uncle Baldo coming in the side porch door with a brown bag full of mushrooms he has picked in the damp woods above the river where Nanticoke Creek empties out into the Susquehanna. After being laid-off from the Buick plant in Flint, Michigan, my uncle came to live with us and take a job in the shoe factories. *"Piecework,"* he'd say, shrugging his shoulders. When he got home from work in the late afternoons, he would climb the foothills out of the valley. He'd walk until the houses below seemed far off, and sometimes he took me with him—showing me how to pick the ones that were good to eat. In the early spring and fall, he'd look for mushrooms.

Part V—Waking Up

In the late summer, especially September, he'd comb the cornfields near the river to pick the leftover sweet corn. They were small, tiny ears forgotten by the pickers. We'd shuck that corn together outside and my uncle would tell me about growing up near Scranton on a farm in the hill country. Then we steamed the fresh-picked corn and everyone got a small ear to eat. Late September corn—the nights chilly, the wind coming on in the maples along the street.

~ ~ ~

The next job I got was working in the EJ shoe factories. It was piecework—packaging shoes—meaning you got paid more if you could pack more. None of the three young guys who were hired with me made our quota that would raise our pay from the $1.80 hourly rate. We weren't fast enough. And by the time we started to get the hang of it—looking at the ticket and pulling the size shoes from different boxes—well, we were having some trouble with the boss. At lunch we'd go with the crew to Ernie's bar about a block from the factory. Ernie would serve up the pasta or soup of the day—usually *pasta e fagioli* (bean and pasta) soup with one thick slice of semolina bread and a glass of beer for a dollar. We had about an hour for lunch, and maybe you could shoot a game of eight ball if there was time. I spent about two months in the packing section before the boss accused two of us of stealing shoes and being late, and he let us go.

In June I went up to the State University in Geneseo to see if I could still be admitted for the fall 1968 term. My old high school counselor had written me a nice letter of recommendation, and the interview went well. I remember driving up there alone in my car, dressed in my "Hong Kong" dark blue suit I'd bought from a tailor at the PX in Danang. The college seemed like a world unto itself, and part of me was excited about the prospects of going to college, like a new start or something different. I saw the dorms and the old buildings where some of the classrooms were, the clock tower on the main campus. It seemed like a world away from where I'd been.

The placement office sent a letter to my home a week later, letting me know I'd been accepted for the fall term. Driving back

33. Slippin' into Darkness

through the Finger Lakes and taking my time, I thought about what I would have to do to get ready for college.

At home again, I knew I had to get a job, something to help me pay for car repairs and the rent I was paying to live with my parents.

~ ~ ~

34

Working Class Hero

We got jobs working concrete for a guy named Gus O'Neal in a small lakeside town. The company was just getting organized, and the pay was good—building foundations for tract homes, prefabs, pouring slabs. Frank would pick me up, and we'd have breakfast at a diner, buy some coffee to go. *"A cup of speed,"* Frank would say. Then we'd smoke before pulling into the boss's house. We'd start doing jumping jacks in the driveway while we waited for the rest of the crew to get in.

The boss and the foreman would be in the kitchen with a few of the local boys, drinking coffee and trying to wake up, pulling at their 7 a.m. hangovers. Seeing Frank and me yelling and slapping hands in the driveway, they peer out not believing it, not knowing what Frank and I knew—we were ahead of them already, making a gig of it—yelling *"Let's go, let's pour it out,"* and making those old country boys wince and tuck into their necks, blinking at us, shaking their heads.

I remember long drives across the state, how the weeks dragged on, and they started to leave us alone, sending us out for cellar-floor jobs, recalls where the finishing crew had messed up, trying to cream it off with a power trowel while the mud was still too wet. And we had to go back and fix it the hard way by hand with a short load of new mud and more hours smoothing it out.

One morning they sent us out to pour a job along Lake Ontario.

It was late October and the leaves pressed down all around us. I remember driving beneath the overhanging trees and the sudden rush that crept in. It was different then for a short while, both of us knowing the job was all this, that we could do it our way. And later, coming out of the basement to smoke cigarettes and shoot cans of

34. Working Class Hero

warm beer the foreman hid in the rear compartment of his pickup, we smiled at each other, the kneepads still strapped on, our faces white with the dust.

On the road below, a family inside a passing station wagon stared at us. And Frank laughed in that cracked, silencing way he had, both of us believing we'd found some turf at last, some working man's hero rap that obscured us, blurring what we really were and what we had seen as if it were behind us, blurred by sweat and work. I don't know exactly why I remember that one day, that October afternoon, why it seems to stand out from all the rest, why it hangs there even now like a smooth field. Something about the roles we assumed, how it blocks out the other days, the times when things didn't go right, the times when we got back too late, tired and drunk from stopping in small-town joints—American Legion bars, hamburger dives, places where a sublime sadness seemed to seep out of the corners—some old man's frustration with the times, the sagging, slow tiredness of growing old. But we were beyond it that day or seemed to be, and high and drunk, choked with work, we waded through all of it, the slow churl of country music lingering, long rides along the back roads.

Another morning in the rain, the boss called it off for the day and we rode around at 7 a.m.—smoking cigarettes, weed, sipping coffee from Styrofoam cups, watching the other folks go off to work or school—laughing at all of them.

~ ~ ~

35

Going Down Slowly

Cal's suicide came as a tremor; it hit me when I tried to look away. An accident, the newspaper said. The obit listed the next of kin, the time of the funeral, his wife's name. It wasn't meant to encourage attendance. It didn't mention his graduation with honors from a university in the Midwest, his graduate degree in photography, or his stint as a salesman for a national company. It didn't say he was a Vietnam veteran. That's the way Cal wanted it.

He was concerned with appearances, with how things should be, with what they should look like. And he was careful; he shunned the vet groups, the rap sessions, the demonstrations. For Cal, it was over.

My friend Frank says that death's a remembrance of all the things you never learned. I never argued with him, but I argued with Cal. One reason his death bothered me so much.

"I write too, you know," Cal had said, the first night we met over dinner. And smirking from behind the clear lenses, his crop of gray hair rooster-like, making an odd downward motion, he'd said, in that raw, raspy voice of his, that it wasn't the war anymore, it was all the things that had happened since. He said it smugly, as if it were his information. I tried to talk with him, tried to tell him that I knew how the war had changed us, how it had filled us with an angry, inconsolable guilt, making us indifferent to the things society believed were important. I tried to tell him we had to let go of ourselves and change. *"We have to help educate people,"* I almost shouted. But it was no use.

And faking the accident, making it look as if he'd tripped over the extension cord and the shotgun had gone off, staging it so his wife could get the insurance money, made it more deliberate.

Cal, Cal. Long fingers curling the bills out, sifting the singles.

35. Going Down Slowly

Smooth, the way they gathered around him. It was how he said things, so you had to listen, pull into him, get closer. He wanted you to look up to him, consider him serious, articulate, artistic. And he was all of those things. He was making a lot of money then and spending it: new Volvos, cameras, cocaine. He'd been married twice before, and Billie was the third. I didn't go to the wedding, but it was a big show. His wife's money, 200 guests. That was May, and by September there was trouble—money trouble, word that his new job wasn't working out. And then Billie not coming home nights. In the early fall, I saw him go into a downtown music store where you could score some drugs.

I wonder what he saw. Black shadows of the leaves, his shirtsleeves turned up, the dogs asleep in the front room. Did he hear the echo of time pulling at him? Was he afraid of things, afraid of embarrassment, of failing? Or breathing hard, did it just hit him and he knew he couldn't keep on, that the force of the blow would ease him back to smoky darkness? Maybe there were geese passing from the swampland nearby, or maybe just the oncoming dark and the circle the back-porch light gave off as he stared at it, the room beyond the screen door silhouetted. Was it peace he turned away from, gasping for air? It must have been other things, too. The constant drumming, the hum—"*The space out back*," someone said, describing an accident, a curve on the road.

Did a distant car startle him, the squeal of tires? Or did he look back and see only his shadow, tall and lean against the shadow of the leaves? He must have thought a long time as he laid the cord out, its bright orange coils unwinding around him. Fifty feet of extension cord and then the trouble light, placed just right on the open tailgate of the station wagon. And then carrying them out, smooth and oily and cold. The smell of the promises they held, the time he'd spent with each one. He must have thought about how to arrange it, practiced it once or twice to get it down. A routine by the time he was gone enough to want it, like he'd wanted other things, to look right. A shout, a clamor, a drumming. Through with caressing himself, curling into tightness. Quick and easy and sure.

Months afterward, when Billie said she'd sold his things—the

Part V—Waking Up

car, the guns, his clothes, cameras, even his books—it lingered. And tonight, as the recent homecoming parade's debris still litters the streets, the big, yellow ribbons sagging, I think about all of it again, and about Cal, strong and sure as the years circling around him. Cal, who knew defeat and despair as tangible things, a tide he could not ebb or endure.

~ ~ ~

36

Be True to Your School

Some things you can never get back. The boy running through the backyards. Running and running. He's jumped hedges and torn through bushes. A smell of begonias and chrysanthemums. Late summer. Crickets early in the afternoon. A quiet hush of cars moving beneath the maples that line the street.

A boy running from his father. The father with his belt out chasing the boy, ready to give him a "licking." The boy disappearing into a backyard full of flowers. A woman there with gray hair watering the rose bushes. The boy hiding behind a giant butterfly bush. Monarchs and swallowtails nearby. The sweet smell of pollen on his shiny blue dress-up pants.

You want to remember that boy—how scared he was that his father would catch him. And the lady, Mrs. Robbins? You raised your finger to your lips to tell her not to give you away. Safe enough until your father passed on the sidewalk; he'd never come into her yard anyway.

He never caught up. He never caught you. The father who is gone now too. And Mrs. Robbins? She told you once about those butterflies. Don't catch them, she'd said, the day she saw you with a net. Some things are meant to be free, to get away. Her house was sold and remodeled. The backyard all garage and patio.

And the boy? That day you ran all the way to the carnival. The James E. Strate's Shows. A dollar to get in. Another five in your snap-up black shoes. Sawdust and barkers calling, *"Hey kid, wanna try your luck?"* And you did. Staring at fat women and snake charmers. Men whacking a platform with a mallet to hit the bell.

Peep shows and animals in cages. Tossing nickels into glass

Part V—Waking Up

bowls. What did you win? A creamer for your stepmother. Some green-glass saucers. Postcards for a nickel. A carnival on the empty fields near Nanticoke Creek. Now just prefab warehouses, self-storage lockers. The bridge is still there. A gas station and quick mart next to the bridge.

You still dream of that creek, the way it moved under the branches toward the river. The trilobites you found there embedded in the flat rocks. A fossil collection you dragged home one by one. The railroad trestle where you and Larry and Greg jumped off into the pools below. How many more summers later?

And what were you running from that day in summer? Was it the anger of that house? The fights and arguments? Was it the mother dead when you were four? The grandfather dead when you were eight? Was it the stepmother and father who could not mouth the word *love*? The brother who was scared and lonely and who listened? Do you remember throwing those fossils at them? The flat stones hitting against the cellar door where they had chased you? Do you remember your own anger? An anger that never went away.

Running became a way to find a few moments away from them. You ran track and cross country. You ran the three miles into northern Pennsylvania and back, the coach calling for you to help the new kid Maury who always fell behind. Maury whose favorite song was "Be True to Your School" by the Beach Boys. Where has he run to now? And Santucco who turned them all around when he almost won the sectionals. Santucco who laughed and laughed at the skinny white boys who thought they were better. Did he slip into history too?

~ ~ ~

37

Homeward Bound

More than 50 years have passed since Ray Munson and I waited in the old hangar at the Danang airfield for a plane to take us out. I don't know what happened to Ray after we got to Okinawa and I caught a plane home after three days and he had to wait for another flight. He was a heavy equipment operator with the battalion.

That night waiting for the plane to take us back stays with me and the confused, anxious feeling we both felt at having come through it all unscathed, our blind pride at having survived blocked out by other things—long lines of other men, Marines mostly, shuffling, waiting. The records check, the orders check. And then Ray coming up beside me in the first glow of dusk, grabbing my arm and asking if I wasn't from his outfit. I'd hitchhiked there, and Ray had one of the guys from motor pool bring him out.

~ ~ ~

38

Where Did You Sleep Last Night?

Somehow, during my second year at the Writer's Workshop in Iowa, I ended up without work and without any money. The loans I had to take out were finished. The job I had with a contractor working at a hospital fell through, and it was December and I needed some money for gas and food until the new term started. Feeling trapped, my friends gone back east until the end of January, I went to the Department of Social Services and asked for some help.

Luckily, the older woman who interviewed me was a veteran too; she was somewhat empathetic, and I got enough money for food and some groceries and it carried me through. But those days were difficult. I was crashing at a friend's place on his couch and he wasn't too happy about that. My other friend had moved out of his apartment to a farmhouse on the Cedar River, and there was no way I could drive out there and back without dropping money for gas. It was the start of the long, dry cold Iowa winter, and I couldn't shake the grayness those days brought and the feeling of loss and loneliness.

~ ~ ~

39

Sweet Melissa

Just as the winter break ended, I got a job at a Texaco Station on the hill above the university, and my friend with the one bedroom decided to rent a three bedroom with a guy from their construction crew. So, they kept a room for me and I paid them with the money from my new job at Bill's station. Bill and I had met the spring before when I'd brought my white Pontiac Catalina into his station to clean the engine after I made a 10-hour haul to Laramie from Iowa City in a 40-mile headwind. Three of us thought we'd try to make California in early March; we gave it up outside of Laramie. I made it back to town, but the motor kept stalling and Bill thought dirt and dust from that headwind had clogged the oil trap in the engine—a thin screen that kept the oil flowing smoothly. He was right; after a couple of flushes that old rig was humming again, and Bill and I were friends. The next spring when I needed work to pay my tuition, he gave me a job.

It was a 50-hour work week, pumping gas and doing oil changes and lube jobs and sometimes small repairs. Bill doled out tabs of anti-asthma medicine every morning. They got you off with a speed-like high made more intense by Bill's coffee, which gave the little pills a trigger. By noon those of us who opened up in the morning were flying pretty high, cleaning windshields and checking oil for everyone. It was a full-service station. On days when I didn't have classes I worked a 10- or 12-hour shift.

I met Nancy that spring, too. She was tall and thin with short cropped blond hair and she had a good laugh. My friend Mary introduced us at a party, and it wasn't long before she was coming up to the station at night near closing time to check out what I was up to.

Part V—Waking Up

The crew called her chatty Nancy because she never talked much at all. I liked her because she played the harmonica and when I asked her to play "Shenandoah" like Odetta did she knew the song right off and hit those notes as if she had a real feeling for things. Back then I was in my Odetta stage. I loved her music more than anything. So, when Nancy knew the Shenandoah song, well it seemed like a good sign.

She'd come up on me from behind and bump into me or just pull at my sleeve. Sometimes she would park her car in front of mine, blocking it and walking off, so that when I came out from the station or from a store, I couldn't leave. Once she even came to my apartment and stood in the doorway and started undressing right there.

Whatever she did, it usually got me going almost as if she knew I'd been reading Flaubert's line: *an infinity of passions can be contained in a few moments like a crowd in a tiny space.* Nancy was always crowding me for space.

The gas station job had its rewards—I got paid in cash once a week and I could work on my own rig after closing—and then I'd bought an old gray 1956 Ford pickup truck with a straight six-cylinder motor that seemed to always need a little work. A couple nights every week Bill would buy whoever didn't have to close up the station some long neck beers and food at a local bar where there were topless waitresses from 5–7 p.m. Those waitresses walked on a platform behind the bar, and Bill liked going there even though he was married with a nice wife and a couple of kids. Later the waitresses would get dressed and they'd have live music, usually someone playing country-and-western hits on guitar. The guys who worked with us were good boys. Not rednecks and not flag wavers either. Sometimes after the bar they'd drop me off downtown at the university so I could hear a reading by a visiting writer. But first we'd sit in Bill's truck and smoke a couple of joints.

The nights I closed up it was different. I shut the lights down first and then I'd go out with the long wooden stick we used to measure the gas that was left in the tanks. You had to keep track by writing down what was left in both the tanks, and then put the

39. Sweet Melissa

numbers in the office logbook. One night in early April the workshop secretary pulled in for gas just as I was shutting down, and I was ashamed at her seeing me in my tan Texaco shirt with the star on it.

It took a good while to get the smell of gas and oil off. I'd wash with castile soap and then the strongest shampoo I could find. I'd always leave the tan shirt and black jeans at the station too, otherwise the smell would settle into the truck's cab and I couldn't get it out.

There's no explaining why things happen the way they do. That's why when Mary called me to say Nancy was in the hospital, I got worried, but I wasn't shocked. Nancy was always a little on edge.

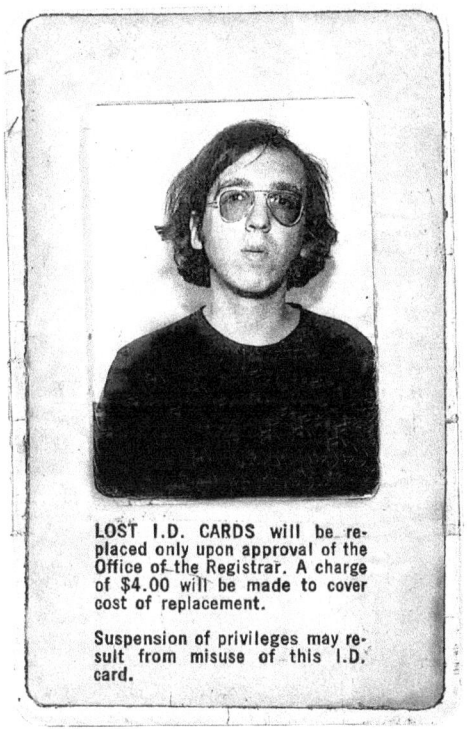

Iowa City, Iowa, 1974. The author in his first year as a graduate student.

"She's in the infirmary at the university hospital," Mary told me. "I think she's freaked out about exams and school."

I didn't say anything. I asked Bill to let me off to go down to see her.

~ ~ ~

Endnote—Off the Road

Listen, Bo. I should never have agreed to tow Nancy's VW back to New York. Bill, my boss at the Texaco station said as much. In fact,

Part V—Waking Up

he said, "You are crazy—you just got your '56 Ford roadworthy. What you wanna tow a car back to New York for?"

Now, I'd like to meet up with Bill again and tell him how right he was about that trip. I'd like to let him know that the taillights we'd rigged up on the tow hitch for the VW went out near Buffalo and I got a ticket from the local cops and had to go that same night to a court to post the fine. It took all the cash I had.

Then, it was after 11 p.m. and I'd been driving since early that morning—nearly 12 hours—well, it started to snow in the hills south of Buffalo. I kept to the back roads hoping I would not get stopped again, and just as I was close to 20 miles from Livingston County and Geneseo—where my friends lived—a car tried to pass me on a downhill grade in the snow, and to avoid an accident, I had to brake hard. The VW in tow jackknifed and pushed the pickup onto the embankment and off the road. There was a dull, thudding clunk and a metal-on-metal crunch. And my pickup was wrecked. State Park Police found me and had my truck towed to a garage in Varysburg—about a mile down the slope. Then they were nice enough to give me a ride to my friend's home. It was 1 a.m.

40

The Other Side of the Sky

    I got my first teaching job by mistake. My friend Judy called me to say she'd seen a job advertised in the local paper. Her husband taught mathematics at the college where the part-time teaching job was. I was putting some numbers up—almost 36 years old and one book of poems to my credit (badly received—one reviewer actually spelled my name wrong). I had the MFA from a fine university and three years directing a workshop inside Attica prison, another two years working in Poets in the Schools Programs and migrant camps and jails. At the interview, the man in charge of hiring new "writing faculty" commented on my open-weave sandals. I was in my first sports jacket, an off-white blazer I'd bought the day before at a mall outlet end-of-summer sale. He was an odd young man—the director of Freshman English with a Ph.D. in Elizabethan Drama from someplace in Ohio. I think his name was Dougson Trust. The chairperson, a plump balding guy in his late fifties, looked at my vitae and kind of harrumphed. I'd brought him a copy of a recent short story publication in a prominent lit magazine.

    "It's not a story," he said. *"Okay,"* I answered, but thought, *"Then what the smoke is it, doctor?" "It wants to be a story, but it's not,"* he'd said.

    "Well," I said, thinking it over, *"they paid me as if it were a story."* Then the writing program person interrupted and asked me to come across the hall to grade some papers—proof that I knew what I was doing. I'd never graded a paper, and I didn't know anything about remedial composition, or Freshman Composition. When he commented on my sandals—huaraches, really—for the second time, I

Part V—Waking Up

told him I had jungle rot on my feet. That seemed to draw the conversation to an end.

I drove home to my rented summer cottage on a nearby lake wondering what I was doing. I had barely gotten in the door when my phone started to ring. *"You've got the job,"* Trust told me. *"And we'd like to hire you to work in our writing lab at night. It will give you a little extra money to supplement the two remedial writing courses you'll be teaching."* His voice sounded like my cat—a thin, throttling purr. I opened up a beer and sat outside on the wooden platform deck that had been built into the side of the hill.

Lake Ontario looked almost calm in the August heat.

Besides typing a fresh copy of my CV for the boys in their blue blazers, my preparation for the interview had been to smoke a thin marijuana cigarette and take my time driving over. An African American playwright friend of mine had shown me how to touch my hair with a little coconut oil as a way of covering up the smoke smell. In those days I lived in a swamp of weed modified by coffee, Camel cigarettes and no sleep. Call it Pot Self-Destruction. Call it a cushion against reality—or a whole new way of starting off the day—skied out at 8 a.m. But what came back then, taking that first job even though it was part-time, I felt like as if I had jumped off a cliff.

I know I'm repeating myself, but it was the same kind of feeling I had with Sgt. Bethlehem my first month in country—every time he took us to the cliffs above Division Headquarters and got us to jump off those sheer cliffs into the South China Sea; a 35- to 40-foot drop into the deep pools below. He was the same guy who kept me from getting killed when I first deplaned in Chu Lai that July of 1966. I was the worst sort of 18-year-old fool you could imagine, and if I'd had my way I might have died my first month there, volunteering for some dumb detail or riding shotgun on dump trucks going off into the surrounding countryside.

The sarge saved me at least twice: interfering with a late-night volunteer recruitment from our tents and cutting me out of orders for a bad line company outfit that had taken a 50 percent loss of casualties in the month before—mostly new guys like me who didn't know where they were yet or what to fear. After almost two months

40. The Other Side of the Sky

at the base, I finally got transferred, but only when the sarge got himself in trouble and was handing out tools from a shed in the company yard. In fact, a lot of us who spent a few months or more at the base near the ocean in Chu Lai got orders to new outfits. My orders were for a combat engineer battalion that would soon be relocating north to Danang.

~ ~ ~

PART VI
Back Stories

41

Going in Circles

    I have always been afraid of cameras, leery of the photographs that seem like small moments detached from time, cut off and tacked into albums. When I visited my Aunt Eleanor in her fifth-floor walk-up in Inwood in New York City, she took out a faded, cardboard album of photographs. It was full of black-and-white snapshots of my brother and me, back from when we were babies and then toddlers. The album was frayed at the edges and the cardboard corners stuck out. One by one she pulled the photographs away from the tiny triangles that held them in place, the pictures she wanted me to have. There were pictures of my mother and father and grandfather that I had never seen before. As much as I distrusted those photographs, as much as I disliked what I thought were contrived poses, quick glimpses of the lives and the people who meant so much to me, I knew what it was my aunt wanted. I knew she was telling me to keep these things, if only to remember who I was, where I'd come from, the people who had made me.

    When she walked me down to the street, we passed the park together—the same park where she'd pushed me in the stroller after I'd been born and my parents had come down with me for a visit. She made me see the park and the river beyond it, pushing me to remember the afternoon in early summer, the stiff breeze blowing uphill, the scent of salt marsh and open water. She showed me the neighborhood where they had all lived once—the church across the street from her building, the tired worn staircases, thick paint and plaster covered over again and again. The neighborhood rose up like a fist, clenched and hard against the years. My Aunt Eleanor stood there trying to slip a twenty-dollar bill into my hand, saying, *"We're leaving*

41. Going in Circles

here soon, you know. Uncle John and Grace and me, we're going over to Jersey down by the ocean. We can't stay here anymore."

She left me at the subway entrance, walked up the block toward Aunt Grace's building. Eighty-one, she walked the five flights three or four times each day, for morning Mass and evening prayers, or to walk to her sister's house or buy groceries. I loved the way she smoked a cigarette and crossed her long, thin legs and smiled when she said my father's name—*Billy*, she'd call him. *"Billy was the oldest boy,"* she'd say, and smile.

Maybe my distrust of photographs arises from the pain that's missing in the ones I remember most. I distrust the things they don't show.

Now whenever I think of my father, I see him standing forlorn and bemused in that way he had, dressed in a jacket and tie on even the hottest days, and I think about what he lived through. I see the town behind it all, the town he raised us in, the job he left Manhattan for, and the house on West Main where we lived with him, not far from the Susquehanna River near the bridge over Nanticoke Creek, the house he bought on the GI Bill, and I see the hills beyond the valley, the mist rising up out of the maples, the distant freight trains like ghosts of summer nights.

I hear them still all these years later—the low moan of engines in the dark—and the sweet, thick smell of the summer river comes back. And I think about one of my father's stories. He didn't have many stories. There were stories about growing up in Hell's Kitchen in New York and carrying tins of beer home for my grandfather. And there were stories about his time in India during the war. The story I remember best was the story he told about the time he'd been forced to bail out of a burning plane into the jungles of Burma. And if you ever met my father, especially in the days when he was in his seventies, he'd tell that story or a clip of it without much prompting. It was a different story than the one he told to my brother and me when we were growing up, but it was part of the same episode, whatever version he gave of it.

Perhaps that is what happens when one tells a story again and again; it is altered each time in a small way, maybe there are more

Part VI—Back Stories

details or fewer, but if one listens to the story more than just one time, it takes on a presence of its own, a reality that doesn't change but grows in the imagination. Some stories take a long time to be understood. It's like the way one sees a painting more clearly after seeing the colors of the country it was painted in, as if landscape and memory made the seeing easier.

It happened during World War II before I was born. The plane was a B-29, and my father was a tech sergeant in charge of payroll attached to the 20th Air Force. They were flying over Burma to their base in India when one of the engines overheated and caught fire. It was late spring 1944, and my father was 35 years old.

After the plane left my father there, dropping into the green of the jungle canopy, he said he remembered seeing the fire engulf the fuselage, the plane going on in a funnel of black smoke. My father always paused when he told it. He had been in planes before, flying as a bombardier with the 13th Anti-Submarine Squadron out of Pueblo, Colorado, in advanced training, but this was the first time he had ever been told to strap on his parachute and get out. I know the co-pilot broke his leg in the jump, and they had to carry him for six days through the monsoon. My father would tell about parachuting into the bamboo grass, about using his machete to cut his way free from the cords of the parachute. It took my father six days to get out of that jungle.

"*We walked out*," he would say. "*We were lucky to make it.*"

He said there was little waiting—one minute they were flying over the green canopy, looking out to the country ahead and then the co-pilot was yelling about smoke and telling them to bail out. At night when my father put us to bed, he told two kinds of stories—stories he made up about my brother and me riding wild horses out west on the prairie, and the other ones that were about his time in India during the war, or about growing up in New York City. We liked his stories because they were an escape, a rare moment when we both got to be alone with our father.

He had been stationed in India, first New Delhi and then Calcutta, and the plane was on a routine run from India to Rangoon and back; part of what was called *the hump*, the flight path from India to

41. Going in Circles

Burma to China. This day they were just hitting the halfway point, what my father called *the point of no return*, when the left engine caught fire. Then they got the word they would have to bail out.

I imagined a rich, green world when I saw it in my mind's eye. And I dreamt of parachutes opening. When we got a little older, my father showed us his Caterpillar Pin and his certificate from the Caterpillar Club that he had received for having bailed out of a plane. He would show us his old flight gear and his machete that folded up. Sometimes my brother and I would pretend we were those fliers down in the basement of our house—in the little room—which had been a coal bin once and now was a storage room of sorts. We would pretend we were lost in the jungle, hacking away at the elephant grass my father had told us about, resting when it got too hot or when we were too tired. He said it was hard going on in the rain, harder still to cut away at the dense undergrowth. I imagined strange birds and snakes, insects—mosquitoes and moths as big as his hands. I wondered about what it had been like to sleep beneath that canopy—another world away from the streets of Hell's Kitchen in New York City where my father had grown up. And I saw my father standing shoulders rounded, head bowed to one side. There was a calm about his face. Even now I see him there—the clothes he has on are the wrong ones for a parachute jump into the jungle—good khakis and brown leather air-wing high tops. He is helping to carry the co-pilot with the stretcher they have rigged up. The night is coming on thick and deep, and there is a kind of pitched camp they have cleared in the brush. They are scared of an enemy patrol, of wild animals, of the wet that clings to them, a penetrating damp that presses in on them with the night growing cooler. After he told us the story, it felt good to fall asleep in our beds with the covers pulled up around us. I know I felt safe seeing my father standing there in the open doorway, looking in at us. I imagined him poised on the lip of the plane, the flames spreading out behind him. My father's world of Burma and of the jungle seemed a long way off—a tiny globe of light and color that was spinning somewhere out of our reach.

When I got older, and after I had come back from my own war, I wrote a poem about the story my father used to tell of his parachute

Part VI—Back Stories

jump. I thought about the fate that had led him home again, only to have his new wife die and leave him with two sons to raise alone, upstate away from his family and friends. The poem was a way for me to connect that war story of his to the life he lived afterwards, where he worked, and the way he treated my brother and me, the almost indifferent way he had with us. I remember his sadness and his anger; the sad way he had of looking out beyond us.

The poem was called:

Rangoon/1944

> After the engines caught fire
> the pilot held it nose up and you bailed out—
> a line of stick men falling into the bamboo grass.
> The co-pilot broke his leg
> and you carried him for six days
> through the monsoon.
> You turned from my bed after you'd told it,
> and before you let the dark in all around us,
> stared, your hands on the open doorway.
> As if for those few moments
> you were above it all again—the house on West Main, the factory downtown.
> As if standing there another life
> still held—
>   spreading like the blossoms of parachutes above a deep green sea.

I have written to the Air Force about my father's parachute jump. I want to know if they can tell me if I am right about the kind of plane it was, if they have a record of the crash. I want all the information that my father could not give me.

I think time distorts things and changes the way we see the past. On my first flight to California in 1966, I was 18 and headed for advanced infantry training and then *south* as we called going to Vietnam back then. My parents drove me to the airport. I was so afraid of getting sick on the flight that I did not have anything to eat the whole trip. It didn't matter. I was nauseous and dizzy by the time we landed in Los Angeles. I still can never ride a plane without thinking about my father's parachute jump. I keep seeing the photograph of him standing with the crew of one of his planes. He is young and handsome, smiling for the camera. I think about the luck, the chance

41. Going in Circles

1st Row L to R: Cpl Keith-1stSgt Eberhardt-1stLt.Bobbitt(Adj)Col Edgar S.Davis(C.O.) Major H.K.Mc Combs, Exec.Officer-SgtMajor NickSperounis-Sgt.Wm J. Mc Carthy.

2nd Row L to R: Cpl Davidson-Cpl Cadigan-Cpl Siegel-Cpl Cangro-Cpl Buffone-Cpl Krause.

Headquarters-Executive and Administrative staff of the 13TH ANTISUBMARINE SQUADRON (H) AAB PUEBLO, COLO

Sgt. William McCarthy and his crew training in Pueblo, Colorado, during World War II, before being sent overseas to India with the 20th Air Force.

that led him to survive his jump and then make his way back to camp only to learn that his mother was ill. They could not get in touch with his other brothers—Uncle Joe was on a ship in the Pacific, Uncle Frank fighting with the Marines at Tarawa, and my Uncle John making his way across France with the army. My father was the oldest, so they sent him back to New York to be with his mother. My father never got back to India. By the time his leave was up, the war was almost over.

I know the past changes us, changing the way we look at the future. I think about the thin thread that links my father and me—like a bridge made of smoke.

~ ~ ~

42

A House Is Not a Home

After he came home from India and the war, my father moved upstate away from the city where he'd met my mother and where he'd grown up. He moved away from his own family and from his old job as a designer/decorator, a job he had before the war. My father was proud of the job he did with the book company he worked for—he would set up the displays for new books. I found one of the pictures he took of a display. It was for the first American edition of Ignazio Silone's *Bread and Wine*. My father had set up all the books in a circle around a red and white checkered tablecloth in the center of the window. On the table he'd placed a bottle of Chianti and a loaf of white bread. I don't think my father had even read the novel, but he was a reader, and I don't think he knew that Silone was from the Abruzzo and not Tuscany, but perhaps Silone would have felt a kinship with my father. They had both come from poverty and they both knew the empty loss of family that adds to the ache of being poor. And my father was simple and direct, blunt when he wanted to be, evasive sometimes too.

What my father had to face and live through and survive would have broken most men. And I don't mean the war. I don't think my father was broken by the sadness he had lived through. Instead, it was work that broke him. Like Silone, he knew the truth of what work was, the long hours and tedium of routine, the feeling of never getting ahead or of finding a way out.

When he came home from the war, my father took a job as a floor sweeper for a department store until my mother's brother got him a job interview at IBM, and they hired my father

42. A House Is Not a Home

in the payroll department as a clerk. He worked there for 26 years.

The house my father bought was built at the edge of town out along the valley floor so you could see the fields across the street and, beyond the fields, the foothills that led up away into the Appalachian Trail. These houses were built during the war for workers. They were well built with sun porches and cool cellars. There were maple trees in front and thick pines in back that must have been there before the houses were built.

It was a good house with a good feel to it. And my father must have thought it was a good place to raise a family. I remember so many things about that house—some of them tied up with my father and his angry, sullen, stubborn way of doing things, and other memories of my mother who seemed to live there so briefly yet whose spirit haunted the place until my father had me put it up for sale.

In those days there was a neighborhood that was growing up around us. I remember the baker who brought us fresh bread at night in the summer, how he stood at our back porch door, making change with one hand and handing over the loaves with the other. He always came at night after he'd finished his work, and my stepmother said he was selling the bread to make a little extra cash; it was bread that would never see the bread delivery trucks or supermarkets. That's why it came wrapped in brown bags. I can never eat any kind of fresh bread without thinking of the summer night he first came to our door, or how it felt to sit in the kitchen of my father's house and eat the thick crusty slices of bread still warm from the oven.

The last time I saw my father's house was in the early spring when I sold it for him and he had moved out. I remember driving back to it alone on a gray day in March. The house was empty of course and I'd had a local painter pull up the carpets so the old oak floors were uncovered and the rooms freshly painted white.

There was a special kind of sadness about the place—a moody stillness that made me want to leave even as I came into it for the last time. The windows were clean and bare in the light. The floors looked

Part VI—Back Stories

The author's father and mother at Watkin's Glen, New York, before they were married, with unidentified young boy on father's lap, mother's friend, and cousins Joan and Elaine Bisio.

pretty good—the varnish still bright even after all the years covered by wall-to-wall carpets. The downstairs seemed like it was bigger than I remembered and I looked into a few of the kitchen drawers, and there in one of the back ones stuck to the oilcloth that lined it was an old ring of my stepmother's.

Suddenly in a quiet, quite unusual way the whole history of my father's house came back again. I thought of the awful sadness the house had seen—first the death of my mother at 38 from cancer, and then my grandfather a few years later. Then later my stepmother's

42. *A House Is Not a Home*

own sickness—her lengthy battle with Alzheimer's. The slow split-up of her own family. Her sisters moving away from her as if they could escape the disease by leaving her alone there with my father. And perhaps that is when it all came sliding at me—the house and the life and the stories it held.

~ ~ ~

43

Estate

My grandmother Adalgisa died four years before I was born. My own mother died when I was four years old, and her father—my grandfather Antonio—died five years after she did. By the time I was in fourth grade all my maternal relatives were dead. My childhood was filled with a very real aura of death and dying, of wakes and funerals, of hushed voices speaking Italian. For years, the Italian language was the language of death, and I confused Italian with adults talking about things I should not hear, and words like *allora* or *aspetta* always made me think something bad was going to happen, that the grownups were pulling away to talk about what my brother and I should not hear. In our house, my brother and I listened from upstairs to the voices of people below us—voices talking in Italian and English, the smells of coffee and anisette, food cooking on stovetops, chairs pulled up to tables. As I grew up the only reminders I had of my mother and grandmother were a few photographs and the books about Italian painting and art that had belonged to my mother.

I knew my grandfather the best of all since he spent a lot of time with me. I spent early afternoons with him, visiting markets, going to the railroad yards where he sold grapes from California to the men who still made wine. Sometimes we'd stop at Eddie's Radiator Repair—the owner was a friend of my grandfather. Today the smell of a car overheating in the summer heat brings me back to that time—to Eddie laughing with my grandfather, offering him a glass of amber wine under an old arbor in back of the shop.

Some Sundays in September we'd pick grapes up along Seneca Lake and I would ride up on the tractor as it stopped and the boxes of grapes were loaded up onto the cart in back. Later, everyone would

43. Estate

sit down to a big meal outside. My grandfather's world was a world of excitement.

But I never knew much about my grandmother; she has remained a mystery. Her name was Adalgisa, though now I know they called her Rae and she died three days after Christmas in 1943. She is buried at Woodlawn Cemetery in the Bronx. When I moved downstate to teach college, I visited her grave in the section called Wild Rose. It's a small, white marble headstone in the shape of the Madonna, wedged on a hillside between two chestnut trees. It was a double plot. My grandfather and mother were buried upstate. When my first-born son Luke died from medical malpractice and hospital incompetence, I buried his tiny coffin next to his great-grandmother. I asked the stone cutter to chisel on her headstone only his first name and the year—1992. He had lived for only 12 days.

The author's grandmother Adalgisa and grandfather Antonio c. 1930s (photograph by Marie Calamandrei).

I know she was born in Recco near Genoa along the Liguria seacoast. I know she came over to America when she was pregnant with my mother. And I know some of what she lived through in those first years. A few years back, I visited my grandfather's hometown in San Casciano in Val de Pesa to get what records I could. I brought his birth certificate, and the clerk in the town office—*the comune*—gave me his marriage certificate. It was the first time I had

Part VI—Back Stories

Antonio and Adalgisa at New York World's Fair c. 1939 (photograph by Marie Calamandrei).

seen my grandmother's whole name—Adalgisa Bisio—and it was the first time I learned where her mother had been born—Lucca. I rolled these new names around; the town clerk took me to another office and introduced me to a man who was the community relations person. He pulled photographs of San Casciano that had been taken during the Second World War.

"I'll show you where your grandfather lived," he said in perfect English. He was an Australian-Italian who owned some vineyards in Tuscany and so he spent his summers there. He walked my wife and our three sons around the town, introducing us to the locals.

Yet, when I look at the few photos I have of her—in one she's in an upstairs window leaning on the sill and my mother is below her posing with her hand on one hip—it's hard to know who she was. I think about going to Genoa, to her town of Recco, not just for the records, but to get the feel of the place, the smells. In another picture I have of her, she is very young, perhaps twenty or so, and she is in a formal black dress and not smiling. The one I like best is the

43. Estate

faded photograph of her sitting on a bench in what looks like a park or playground. She never became a United States citizen and there is a youth and resilience in her face.

The author's grandmother Adalgisa as a young girl c. 1904.

44

Dedicated to You

My mother's story runs its thread all through the house on West Main. It lingers in the cellar where my grandfather had a small bar to talk with his friends, and lies stacked and forgotten in her art books, in the large folio edition of *The Divine Comedy*, in all the papers of hers my father threw away after he remarried. My mother's story seems the most important one to me, and I know very little about her life, especially her youth and the years before she met my father. She died on a sunny day in June in her 38th year.

My mother moved out of the Bronx in New York when she took a teaching position at Triple Cities College, a spin-off of Syracuse University during World War II; eventually it became Harpur College and SUNY Binghamton and now Binghamton University. But for my mother it was work that made her move upstate and it was her father's friend who helped her get a place to live there.

My grandfather's friend, Giudice Mastro, was from the Puglia in Italy, and he had moved out of New York to work as a consultant for the fledgling International Business Machines. My grandfather met him in New York City, and they had become fast friends. As I look at the photograph of my mother and father at Watkins Glen before my parents were married, I see how young they both were—how their youthful innocence could not have prepared them for the losses that would follow. Searching for some record of my mother's education, I stumbled upon a Hunter College notice from 1938: there under Prize Awards for Italian as a major course of study is an Honorable Mention and my mother's name. And I think of what my life and my brother's life might have been like had she lived longer, even until we were in our teens.

44. Dedicated to You

I think how my father might have been different too, how his own dreams must have been lost when she left him alone with two sons to raise, upstate, away from his New York City roots and his own family. I do not have clear memories of my mother. There are scenes, images I can't forget. But none of them seem real, like blurred photographs, glimpses of our life together, but nothing more. They are fragments, shards of pottery from a thick vase that will not fit together, will not find a shape.

One is an image of my mother and father lying close together on the couch in our living room. My grandfather is bouncing my younger brother Dennis up and down on his leg. There is laughter and my father and mother are smiling.

The other memory is when my brother and I visited my mother in the hospital. She is lying back on the pillows and her face is flushed with the heat, her hair dark against the whiteness of the pillows and the sheets. She is smiling at both of us as we come into the room. I remember walking into the room and seeing her sit up, push herself up to reach out her arms to us. My father lifts us and she pulls us close to her. She smells like lilacs

The author's mother Marie as a young girl in the Bronx.

and sweat and salt. The windows are open and there is a breeze. Is this an imagined memory? Have I recreated it in my mind? It seems cut off from other things. Or is it a memory I created, filling in the edges with reason and imagination? I know it was summer, she died in June, and I remember that hospital room and the white glare of the day.

There's a sense of the season changing, thickening with heat. Time seems like a hand stirring the ripples in a pool. I cannot remember her voice.

In memory there are moments that seem to fill the screen, but perhaps they are instead what Pavese knew—*only moments*—cut off from the whole of the experience and like fragile blossoms their scent seems to come and go.

After that visit, we never saw my mother again. And now, all these years later, the memory does not go away and does not sharpen, but remains there like that shard of pottery, broken and fragmented, impossible to be put back together, to congeal or take shape.

45

Sometimes I Feel Like a Motherless Child

After my mother died, nothing in our lives was ever the same again. Whatever we did, wherever we went, whether it was to a park for a picnic or to a friend's home for dinner, there was always the sense of something missing, or voices behind the conversation that intoned of her absence in polite whispers and stares. Her death had changed us and altered the days and nights. There was a kind of empty, hollow space, and I think an essential part of me was lost forever.

And in that first full summer when I looked out at what seemed like my world at the time, I began to see the house on West Main beneath the towering maples, the empty field across the street glazed with the first wash of summer dark, the slow freights passing through the West Endicott yards, the redolent distant river smells, and the cool crisp nights in the valley.

Young as I was, I began to see the breadth and limits of the place, to glimpse in a grownup way how deep the change in my life was, how the feeling would not leave. Then I did not understand the significance of things, only a penetrating loneliness. All these years later, it came to me one night as I told my wife, Michele: *"You know I think all this time I have been afraid of people taking things from me, and now I realize it was just losing my mother."* Now this seemed like such a mundane observation, but it had a profound impact on me, that sudden recognition.

When the summer flattened out, the days grew hotter, and the leaves on those maples were full and heavy. It felt as if a hand had stirred the water in a pool, ripples widening out and the nights and

Part VI—Back Stories

Left to right: The author and brother Dennis with mother and father c. 1951, less than a year before mother's death (photograph by Antonio Calamandrei).

days became a blur. I did not understand the significance of the loss, only the feeling of being adrift and alone.

That same summer my uncles and aunts from New York City came up to help my father and my grandfather take care of my brother and me. In the family pictures there is a sense of movement, of one or two appearing and then reappearing.

This is when the real trouble began and when I realized my mother was really gone. And this is when my father began to tell us his stories, when he began to put us to bed each night after we had been with the housekeepers or the babysitters who came in the morning when he left for work and left when he came back at night. The dark seemed to come early, like a sudden rush of wings or a shadow passing overhead.

45. Sometimes I Feel Like a Motherless Child

The first housekeeper was a woman who lived in a gray house in an old neighborhood on the south side of Johnson City only five or six miles from our home. She was a stout, round-faced woman with arms like thick clubs and she seemed very nice on the day my father and my grandfather took us to her house for a visit. She made us come inside to sit down and offered us some freshly baked muffins with raspberry jam and she looked at my brother and me and smiled. And this woman and her home have stayed with me because it was the first visit, the first time. I remember her gray dress and how the white sleeves stood out from her shoulders, winglike and stiff. She had iron-gray hair and her eyes were dark, questioning.

If her house was still there, I could find my way back to it even now, even after all this time. I could find the street, the house set back from the curb with a short concrete sidewalk leading to the front porch, its gray asbestos shingles streaked with age, cracked and blistered by the sun. The front steps cinder block with concrete poured over them, thin iron pipes as handrails. It was the first of many visits we would make to arrange housekeepers or babysitters, and some trips took a lot longer than the first one. She only lasted a week or two and then one night, when my father came home from work, she told him she had to quit.

And there was a string of housekeepers/babysitters—sometimes Edna, our next-door neighbor, at other times a woman who might stay for a week or two—until finally, my father met Norma who lived outside of Binghamton in the farm country near Pennsylvania. I remember the day we picked her up at the farm, the ride into the countryside, the deep green of the fall fields and the smells of the farmyard. Norma came back home with my father and my grandfather. And they both seemed to like her right off. She was energetic and talkative, and in less than a month we both were in school—I was in kindergarten and riding the public bus to school, the bus stop 50 feet from our home. My brother was in a half-day nursery school near our home.

What's hard about memory is that it plays tricks on you, or as a college friend of mine said, *"We don't remember the past, we disremember it."* I guess he meant that we reinvent what happened so that

Part VI—Back Stories

it seems better than it actually was. I have never really wanted to face some of the memories of my own childhood, yet today while repotting the rosemary bush I began to think about what happened to me and to my brother after the summer was over.

The first thing was the short and difficult episode with Norma. After a couple weeks, Norma did not always go home on the weekends, then one day my father said he had asked Norma to marry him. I didn't quite understand what this meant, but my father seemed relieved when he said it. After Norma moved into my father's room, the trouble started.

One day I had an accident at school. I went in my pants and I was afraid to tell anyone what had happened, so I sat with the smell for the lunch hour and then all the way home on the bus. As I got off the bus, the driver laughed.

"Hey, kid you got a load on, huh? Better change your pants when you get home."

When I got back to our house, Norma was there and she was angry that I'd had another accident.

"I'm so sick of changing kids with their pants full of shit, diapers full of shit, kids who can't wipe their asses. I hate the two of you."

Then she slapped me across the face and dragged me upstairs to the bathroom and pushed me into the tub, still yelling and angry. I was almost five years old then. I remember her yellow housedress with a blue pin on it and her hair pulled back off her forehead.

I had a lot of accidents. I think I was scared, worried, nervous at what was going on. Norma left that fall; the police came to our door to get her things. It was a bad scene—my father and grandfather were both there. My brother was crying.

~ ~ ~

46

Hurt

The next housekeepers were also live ins: the mother's name was Elizabeth and her daughter was Barbara. They came highly recommended by a friend of my father's and for a few weeks it was all right. She and her daughter slept in my grandfather's room while he was away on one of his trips. I remember how her daughter Barbara made us come into bed with her before we went to school while her mother was downstairs and my father had left for work. She gave us pieces of hard candy she kept under her pillow if we promised not to tell. My brother and I both knew we wanted the candy, especially before breakfast. It was sticky and sweet. We ate the candy while Barbara slept a little longer. The room smelled of mint and witch hazel, and the shadows of the maple trees outside drifted across the room. Later in the months that followed, Barbara asked us to let her do things for the candy. Our lives seemed tied up with these strangers who were not even kind to each other. Sometimes our neighbor Edna would stop by and ask about us. She'd stand in the kitchen in the midst of a fight between Barbara and Barbara's mother Elizabeth. She'd cradle us in her arms. If we were lucky, Barbara might take us in the backyard after school while she sat on the back stoop, chewing gum.

~ ~ ~

The first light comes in through the blinds, a stark white light fractures the dark in the room, the double bed. I can hear the sound of the wind outside, the noise of passing cars on the street. Someone is next to me in the bed. It takes 40 years for me to realize who it was—a girl,

Part VI—Back Stories

maybe 16 or 17. Long brown hair. She gives me candy—sweet, hard candy. I like the taste of the candy. I still remember this taste—lemon and butterscotch. Her name is Barbara. She is the daughter of the housekeeper who lives in with us.

These are really the first live-ins besides Norma. My younger brother is in his crib in the other bedroom. I realize I am crying, the tears seep out of me. I am not in my own room; I sleep in the room with my younger brother. I have a single bed. I feel her hand on my forehead. Here, she says and unwraps another piece of hard candy. Sweet, so sweet. I am propped up on a pillow in the bed and she reads me a story. It's a story with yellow ducks. Tiny yellow ducks on a pond. There are clouds above the pond.

Someone calls. Someone calls for the girl to get up out of bed. There is shouting, the girl pulls back the sheets and gets up. I hear my brother crying in the other room. And then I hear the other voices, too. It's time for your enema, she says. I am in the bathroom and she puts the plastic tube up inside of me, squeezing the red bulb to push the liquid into me. It hurts. And then I say—It hurts. Elizabeth, Barbara's mother, says—Just sit there now. Sit still.

Later, back in the bedroom in the double bed, Barbara whispers. Hush, she says, hush.

Under my pillow I can feel the candy wrappers. I feel her hands. Her breath. When I was almost five years old, my father began hiring a string of housekeepers and live-ins to take care of my younger brother and me. Most of them didn't last too long. One of the housekeepers was named Elizabeth and she brought her daughter Barbara with her. The sexual abuse began sometime after they came to live with us and lasted until I entered 1st grade. I remember waking up to the smell of candy.

~ ~ ~

One night my father came home early from work and walked into the midst of a fight—Elizabeth whacking my brother for wetting his diaper while I stood there crying. They were gone the next day. I watched a taxi come to pick them up. My father stayed with us

46. Hurt

for a couple days or maybe it was the weekend and he didn't work. I know he talked with Edna, our neighbor, and they worked something out until my father could arrange for another housekeeper. This time a friend of Edna's got involved, and this proved to be an important change.

~ ~ ~

Part VII
Falling Forward

47

In a Sentimental Mood

How I Met Your Mother

We met in the fall of the year after I'd been hired to teach two sections of remedial English and work in the college writing lab for another eight hours every week. I was living on Lake Ontario then in a summer house that we had to vacate by the late fall. There was no central heating. I was living with a woman who was a painter turned photographer. Around the same time we moved—early October—I went to a talk by Gloria Emerson at a downtown veterans' conference. I had met Gloria Emerson in 1976 at the Peace Bridge in Buffalo when a group of veterans and activists walked Bruce Beyer back from his exile in Canada. They arrested him once he got to the American side of the bridge (Ramsey Clark was his defense lawyer), but they locked him up anyway. Twenty, maybe thirty of us—grassroots veterans against the war—had come up to walk Bruce Beyer home from Canada. Beyer was a draft resister who had chosen to go to Sweden and then Canada after being arrested with other war protesters in a Unitarian church in Buffalo. He fled his three-year prison term. They took him into custody as soon as we entered the United States. Emerson came up to me out of the crowd that was milling around the U.S. Customs office. (See The Buffalo Nine, http://en.wikipedia.org/wiki/The Buffalo Nine)

"*Good to see those VVAW buttons (Vietnam Veterans Against the War) and those jackets after all these years,*" she said.*

I nodded and watched her walk away—a tall, gangly woman in a

---

* In the year it took for Bruce Beyer to deal with the charges against him, we became friends and stayed friends until his death in June of 2019.

47. In a Sentimental Mood

gray trench coat trailing cigarette smoke. My friend Conrad, who'd been an Army medic in Vietnam, laughed—*"You know who that was, man? Emerson,"* he said, *"Gloria Emerson."* He gave me a copy of *Winners & Losers* when we got back to his home later that day. They let Bruce Beyer go for a short while, but eventually he did 11 days in prison.

Six years later in Rochester, New York, in October of 1982, I went to hear her speak at a fundraiser for an upstate veterans center. I had read her book and it had changed me. Up until then, only Robert Jay Lifton's *Home from the War* had really made an impression on me. But as I read Gloria Emerson's *Winners & Losers*, I knew it was a book that brought us—especially as veterans—face to face with our own country, its shortcomings and its failures. It was as if reading her words and the words of those she interviewed, we could at last *come home*. There seemed to me both truth and solace in that book. As one man said to her: "Vietnam was a dead end for most of our best hopes and purposes.... We need to free ourselves of the bitterness and heal what we can of the hurt—not to forget, but so we can remember and use the memories and the learning to save lives and strengthen what decency we can find. The aftermath of the war has been like a long and terrible grieving for someone we loved, a crippling kind of grief that is hard to get beyond...." She knew the veterans and in the knowing she became a kindred spirit. At last it was all right to admit what had happened. I remembered her touching my old field jacket that day in Buffalo. It was all right to be who we were.

"What's your name?" she asked when I approached her after her talk and asked her to sign my copy of her book. *"It's good you have the hardcover edition of my book,"* she said. *"It has the list of dead by state—they cut that out of the paperback."*

I turn to those pages now and see the list, staring at New York: 4,033, Pennsylvania: 3,066, Texas: 3,316. I think of the friends I lost. That's how her book hits you—personally. I told her my name. She grabbed hold of me and said she knew my poems about the war. *"A veteran sent me your book in the mail,"* she said. I was surprised she knew my poems, but also a bit doubtful. Her inscription read: *"For*

Part VII—Falling Forward

Gerald, whose poetry, much of it is engraved in the heart of Gloria Emerson."

I couldn't afford the $100-a-plate dinner that was to follow her talk. I thanked her and said goodnight. A few days later, I got a package in the mail—it was a copy of Gareth Porter's book, *Vietnam: A History in Documents*. Her introduction to the book included a few lines from one of my poems. I should have known better than to not believe what she'd said; that book was her way of proving it. I wrote back to thank her for the book and we began a correspondence that lasted until the 1990s. Gloria was always giving me advice—back then I really needed it—as the singer Gil Scott-Heron wrote: "Good advice is sure enough hard to come by." The end line from one of her first letters is a quip and a metaphor: "Don't be impressed anymore by the wall-to-wall carpets, please."

Later that fall, a week before I had lunch with your mother for the first time, I got a call from Gloria with an assignment. Veterans Day in Washington, D.C., Gloria had managed to get me a job writing an article for the *National Catholic Reporter* on the dedication ceremony for the new Vietnam Veterans Memorial in Washington designed by Maya Lin. The editor of the newspaper, Tom Fox, had been a stringer for the *New York Times* in Vietnam and he knew Ms. Emerson very well. She told me over the telephone: *"You have to go down there and cover the dedication ceremony and then you'll write a poem about it later. That's why you need to go. First you get paid to write about it and that will cover your expenses. Do you have a credit card?"* I laughed.

I borrowed some cash from a friend and took two other veterans with me—one drove his car. Gloria arranged a *pied a terre* in Washington about 10 blocks from the memorial that gave me a place to sleep and where I could write the article. It was due 48 hours after the Veterans Day parade and ceremonies. It rained for two days while we were down there. We'd all grown up with the rain. The article was titled "I got paid $400, an amount that almost covered all the costs. The poem I wrote in stages over the next eight months, and after many exchanges with Gloria and Reginald Gibbons (the editor of *TriQuarterly*), the poem "The Hooded

47. In a Sentimental Mood

Legion" was eventually published in the Winter 1984 issue of the magazine. When it appeared, Gloria called me on the telephone. *"You know,"* she said, *"you've lost one poem in writing another."*

On a Monday the week before I left for Washington, your mom and I went out for lunch at Don & Bob's on Monroe Avenue in Pittsford. We didn't really know each other then—just from English Department meetings—and we immediately got into a disagreement over a famous writer. I called her attitude about the man ignorant and we were off into an argument. I guess that's characterized our relationship for many years—we can argue about anything. When she asked me if I were Irish, I told her no, not really, I had almost been first generation Italian—my mother had been born in the Bronx a few months after my grandparents emigrated from Genoa, Italy. Your mom always says she immediately knew she could talk to me when she was realized I was an Italian in disguise.

We went back to work at the college and I didn't see her again until the winter months—after my article had come out in the newspaper and after I'd begun work on the poem. I had found a house in your old neighborhood in Rochester that was closer to the college and pretty reasonable. And by the end of my first year teaching and the start of my second, we had become friends; and that was all. It took almost another year before we fell in love.

~ ~ ~

And then there's the article I wrote so I could write the poem Gloria wanted me to write.

It's called:

"Their Names Are Everywhere, All Places, We Carry Them Everywhere We Go...."

Washington, D.C.—November 1982

I don't remember seeing it the first time. There were details: faces, a park service volunteer who asked if I needed help, small flags in front of some of the panels. I had to go away from it, back into the trees. It became a black wedge, a blur.

Two Lakota Vietnam vets stopped me to ask if I knew where it

Part VII—Falling Forward

was, "Our black scar," they said smiling. One of them shook my hand, I pointed to the right.

Below the hill, there was a concession stand, a small lake, ducks. I drank coffee, shivering. Three veterans sat together around one of the metal tables.... They said they'd camped out the night before, you had to get far enough back into the trees. One of them, a black-haired Southerner, had a long scar that ran down his left cheek. He stared at me. It was probably the jacket I had on—the one my sarge had given me in Chu Lai, his Korean War jacket that looked like an officer's coat but was really meant to have a cold weather liner. They must have thought I was an officer.

When I went back again, it had changed. There were more people, television cameras. Three men were taking pictures of each panel. I could see it clearly now. The wall of names. Markers without graves, some said later. The crowd thinned out—a dampness refracted from the slabs. As I walked deeper into the center, the new sod was spongy, oozing. It felt like walking into a gigantic wound, a wound in ourselves that needed more than just recognition and reconciliation. It needed some truth about who we are and what we have become.

I found the name my friend had asked me to look up—John Joseph Ugino, 34 East, Line #1. Later, I found the other names I knew where there, but I didn't find the one I was looking for, I didn't expect to. I didn't find him in the faces that stared back at me either. And I saw it close up for the first time. The others were there.

That evening we went to a salute to Vietnam veterans and the DAR Constitution Hall. We listened to the music. My friends wanted to stay and hear Wayne Newton. I went outside on the stone steps and smoked a cigarette. Two guys who said they were Vietnam veterans told me I needed *identity*. One of them offered up a plastic box with a pin inside: the pin said "Vietnam Veteran" and had a map of Vietnam in its center. *"The Vietnam Brotherhood Association,"* his brochure read. *"Wear this pin close to your heart. It's a positive image. Identify yourself as a Vietnam Veteran."*

"We need identity," he was saying. "It's only seven bucks today. We usually sell them for $10." He told me it was what I needed, that

47. In a Sentimental Mood

he could see I was depressed like a lot of the brothers who had seen the monument.

"You need pride," he said. "You need to identify yourself, man." I told him I knew who I was.

It was different at night. The reflections of the streetlights were the only illumination. There were no floodlights yet. A mist hung over it. You must see it at night. It was more personal then, more intact. Your own face was hidden from the glare, the flash of cameras, the stares.

At midnight, a group of veterans from a hospital in Mead, South Dakota, held a vigil—a ceremony of sorts. Their leader, a man named Vern, spoke about their trip, the candles they lit to bring back to the ones who could not make it. I followed them and read more names. As I walked away from it again, the candles were spread out along the walls. That was the first day.

On Thursday, I met Fred. I went to the ceremony in Arlington at the tomb of the unknown soldier. It was different there. The dead were there in among the stones.

You could see the leaves blowing over the graves. I listened to the cheers as Caspar Weinberger said, "We will never again ask our soldiers to participate in a war we do not intend to win." Something was wrong. I watched a security guard try to get a group of veterans to remove a banner from the rail—it read "Vietnam Veterans of America." They told them to take it away. It was still there as I left.

Veterans Day was the first time I heard some call it a *wailing wall*, the East Wall, the one I was most familiar with. And there was trouble that day. A Black Vietnam vet was shouting, "We're still fighting, what are we fighting for?" There were angry veterans who yelled for him to shut up. "The war is over," they said. I stood watch in the crowd. I watched the children climbing up on the polished stone. It was warm and the dampness that had been there the night before was gone. In the sunlight you could see the names clearly.

I came back to it again in the evening. I could hear someone crying. "Man, this is it. We're really home now. We've come home at last."

"It's unnecessary," his friend told me, "he's drunk."

Part VII—Falling Forward

And there were other groups of veterans there that night. Someone playing a guitar, singing "Freedom's just another word for nothin' left to lose." Two veterans in camouflage jackets were drinking beer and pitching the bottles into a paper sack. I watched the visitors pass by. A girl stops her jogging and walks toward it. I can hear the noise of traffic from the street above.

And I see the wreaths again, the medals, the fragments of the things we carry with us, the tiny flags. A Marine veteran has stolen a flag from a government building. He stands holding it out on a makeshift pole at the apex of the two walls. He will not leave until the ceremony on Saturday. That night I found another name. A woman offered me her plastic pocket flashlight. A guy from boot camp and then advanced training, the first time I came through Washington on my way home.

Fred was there when I got back. We were camped out on the slope in front of the monument. There were more veterans. Someone is arguing. The music has grown louder. Fred leans over and bums a cigarette. For the first time, I notice his metal crutches spread out in a vee behind his sleeping bag. He lost his right leg near Chu Lai in 1966. "Another jarhead," he says and laughs. We smoked cigarettes and stared at the flag, the gold fringe throwing odd reflections on the black walls.

"I'd like to blow it out," he told me later. He wanted to use an M-79. And although I knew he was drunk then—he'd been drinking for a while—I knew what he meant. I knew we should get angry with it—no, not the names of our dead, but with the lies they were dragging in here. The lies that would play out all weekend long.

In first light, the veteran was still holding the flag. Someone else was curled up in a sleeping bag in front of it. We were sprawled out on the wet grass—five of us. We were home here, sleeping in full view of all of them.

That morning we walked uptown for coffee. Fred wanted to talk and we stood for a good long while along Constitution Avenue. I watched the faces of the drivers as they passed. Fred has his back to them. He is balanced on one crutch, smoking a cigarette, poised like some graceful bearded crane above the sidewalk.

47. In a Sentimental Mood

That day we all became more exposed. A group of Vietnam Veterans Against the War started a dialogue with the crowd. A shouting match developed. The police moved in almost too quickly. Angry veterans told the police the war was over. One man tried to get to the speaker, threatening. Others shouted, "This is not the place for it." There was hate here, the raw, angry, open kind of hatred. I thought about the reasons for the ceremony—to reconcile our differences. A live TV camera crew caught it all. I walked away again.

In the late afternoon, it began to rain. The reading of the names of the American war dead went on at the National Cathedral. For the first time, I thought about going home, about what I was doing there. At dusk, the rain began falling harder. Everything about it had changed again. I could hear the noise of the generators as they whined away. The floodlights gave the walls a shattered look. The names were blurred by tiny rivulets of water. They had put up snow fences to keep tomorrow's crowds back from the soft turf. I saw the names that were not there, the names of the ones who had died since—from Agent Orange or the other more deliberate ways.

I hitched a ride to the Washington Hotel where the Marines were celebrating. Fred was there, sitting on a couch against the wall.

"I knew you'd be back," he said. Broken beer bottles were strewn on the deep carpets.

Behind us, voices were singing the hymn together.

Inside the barroom of the Washington Hotel, the Marines were drunk again. Fred smiled. "Write a good story," he said.

A tide of submerged violence was all around us, a nightmarish thing that could not be controlled.

"We're exposed now," he said. "We're like the snail that has eaten its own shell, we hurt easily. Now, we start fighting ourselves." I left him there and walked out into the rain again.

I was soaked through when I got back to it. I guess this was how I wanted to keep seeing it, streaked with rain, standing out in the glare of the floodlights.

Saturday morning. Through the sunlight, the cold seemed unnatural. Spectators yelled "Welcome home." Some veterans saluted, threw up their fists. I joined a group of Black veterans

Part VII—Falling Forward

holding a banner for social justice. That was all I could do. I walked with them for three blocks. While I waited for the dedication ceremony to begin, a Black Vietnam vet with a portable microphone tried to speak about unemployment, medical benefits, veterans' rights. The crowd circled him, and two cops on horseback broke through, chasing him, forcing him away from there.

The crowd cheered and a tall ex-Marine shouted, "Leave him here, we'll take care of him." The crowd, the majority of them Vietnam vets, laughed and cheered again. I watched as the Black vet was pushed outward toward the Washington Monument and the lake. A man with two sons in tow looked at me—"Did you hear that?" he asked his sons.

As I walked toward Constitution Avenue again, I could barely see it. The crowd was growing, spreading back. The once empty bleachers were filled with people. There was music playing. I could hear a voice—"Thank you America, thank you for remembering us."

On the street, Fred was drinking a beer with an ex-Marine from Massachusetts. I told him about what had happened. Fred turned away. His companion, Morris, said, "Easy man, we need to educate ourselves. We don't know things about our own history. For some guys this is the beginning."

I told him it was the beginning of something else.

The wall is up. The dedication ceremony is over. The snail has eaten its shell. The truth is there—exposed in its own way—on the cluttered floors of the hotels, in the broken glass and crushed out cigarettes. But it is not my kind of truth, or Fred's, or many of the others who did not come to Washington. There *is* hope in that.

When the snow falls silently past these names of men and women, maybe the veterans who stayed away will come back to haunt this place. Maybe we will find ourselves again, the men and women we might have been, they could have been. Their names are everywhere—rising like *a single black wing above a grassy place. Their names are everywhere, all the places that were them.*

November 1982

~ ~ ~

47. In a Sentimental Mood

Father and Son

Now what comes back about Gloria Emerson is the next spring when she came up to speak at the college where I had taken a job teaching composition and creative writing. She gave two talks: one in the late afternoon to a packed crowd of undergraduate journalism majors and some faculty, the other in the evening to an even bigger group in a large auditorium. Later we had dessert at the chairperson's house. I listened as they argued with Gloria about her politics.

In the morning over coffee at the airport she told me, "You and men like you have a chance you know; you could be good fathers, and

Walking Bruce Beyer home from his exile in Canada with other anti-war activists and members of Vietnam Veterans Against the War (VVAW). Note Gloria Emerson on left (against the rail) behind Beyer and his father, in center Mary Ann Smith with sunglasses and purse, and further back to the right of Ms. Emerson is a head shot of author with aviator shades. Furthest back are members of VVAW Livingston County Chapter (left to right with beards): Paul S., Carl M. and Conrad B (Don Dutton, *Toronto Star*).

Part VII—Falling Forward

you can be better fathers than your fathers were to you. Because of what you've seen and been through—you have a chance."

So how is this about you? Well—just those words of hers. I think I tried to live up to what she was saying—although I'm not certain I pulled it off—but I think I tried to be a better father than my father was to me. What's hard about time is that you cannot go back and erase the mistakes you make—you can only go forward, try harder, think about the choices you have, what you can do.

for Nicholas

~ ~ ~

48

Winter in America

> Off the Count—*Letter to James Baldwin from a place in my memory* or *Winter in America*—Gil Scott-Heron

You drop in as if you've come over the landscape in a parachute. It's as if you are about to land on another planet—but it's not another planet—just Wyoming County, upstate New York. A fortress, a castle, its shadows looming over all—desolate, standing apart from all the countryside that surrounds it—and like its brother Angola State, it is the living, breathing skull of a system gone awry, a system bent on punishment and recidivism and the racist laws that perpetrate this system—a penal colony worse than Kafka's—built on pillars of salt and blood.

Attica.

You see those back roads in winter—two lanes with snow piled three feet high on each side—in fall on those gray, rain-filled days, you remember the snow as you pass through towns with names like Perry, Pike, Trout, Clinton Corners and Darien; towns whose names stay with you. They linger with their old Main Streets and boarded-up storefronts, coffee shops and cafes where recruiters go to buy breakfast for local boys who are thinking about enlisting. Those towns give way to fields and farms.

When you land there's just the walls—a gigantic tomb with slanted walls like an ancient fortress—immense, gray, standing like Ozymandias. A god of death. A stark gray obelisk. You feel small as you go inside, and you have to shrink yourself, tuck your neck into your shirt or coat.

First, there are the physical things: the towers, the stone walls, the gates, the series of entrances, the electric locks, the regular locks,

Part VII—Falling Forward

the keys—so many keys that even today the sound of keys jangling still makes me think of jail and the jailers. There is the stone coldness of the place—a sense of entering a huge stone cathedral with low ceilings. Unlike the breadth and depth one feels inside the old cathedrals of Italy, Attica makes you feel small, dwarfed, channeled into a series of corridors and entrances. Even the entrance is chopped up, confused, disorienting. The front gate guards calling out "One coming in."

And then there are the searches, the screenings, the emptying of pockets, briefcases, bags. Next, the metal detectors with the officers staring, the long series of steel gates, the keys, the locks. The way you have to stoop—the feeling in your neck as if there were a pressure pushing down on you, an enormous pressure forcing you to hunch up, a feeling akin to being in a pit and time's pendulum is swinging down at you—cutting you with its razor-sharp blade—as if the whole weight of the walls, the tiers and steel were closing in on you, inside.

~ ~ ~

Now, with the murder of George Floyd and the revitalization of the Black Lives Matter movement, I realize what I learned during my time teaching inside Attica in the 1970s was more important than anything else I have ever done or witnessed.

I have written this piece and torn it up six or seven times trying to get it right, trying to understand how I could explain why it is important for me as a white male and why it has become a central event in my own life, shaping my reading and actions.

And I should have sent this letter to you while you were still alive and I had just turned 30 years old, but back then I was too full of anger and frustration, too ill-informed, too full of my own problems. And I was afraid of what you might say or not say, but now I know you would have had something to say. I had to grow up first. I had to read a great deal more, and I had to lose my firstborn infant son as well. Now, I can write honestly and truthfully about what I learned in those years teaching a writing workshop at Attica prison. As you know there is a difference between honesty and truth. It's just taken me a long time to understand the difference.

48. Winter in America

~ ~ ~

When I was 29, my friend and former undergraduate professor got me involved in teaching a workshop in creative writing inside Attica prison. I was fresh out of graduate school, had no job prospects and didn't know what I wanted to do. He suggested I come in on a Saturday morning and check it out. Now I realize he was kind of *tricking me* into it, taking over his class at Attica; a class he had begun as part of a community service thing off a poetry fellowship he'd received from New York State.

My first trip inside was in June of 1976, and I read some of my own poems to his class of seven or eight men. On the way back to his home, my friend suggested I take over the class for the summer while he went out to Michigan with his family. He knew I would see for myself what prison was like, and I learned a few things that first summer. It was the start of an experience that would change me and my life forever; what some now call a *defining* moment.

There was a stark difference between the conformity of graduate school and teaching a writing workshop in Attica prison. When I attended graduate school, there were no Black people at all—no professors and no graduate students in the workshop. In my second year, one Black woman was finally admitted.

I felt at home in the company of the men at Attica: they could read you, could see through your weaknesses and read your strengths. It wasn't too long before the make-up of my class changed, enlarged; guys wanted in and the prison authorities let the class grow.

I had never felt at ease in graduate school. I felt isolated, alone, and I probably brought it on myself: my professors there, especially in my first year, kept trying to bag me—"Have you ever read George Oppen? You are writing like him," one said. Back then, I had not read Oppen, but I knew what they wanted and felt I had to conform. This notion about conforming left me in my first summer teaching the workshop in Attica prison; I felt as if I could do what I wanted to do; I could tell the truth and be honest with the men in my class. And equally important, they knew I was not coming in for the money;

Part VII—Falling Forward

they could tell from my clothes that I didn't have a lot of money. They knew.

By the fall when my friend came back from Michigan and said, *"Go on, take the workshop, I'm teaching full-time as it is,"* I still wasn't sure what I wanted to do, but already I had begun to understand a few things about prison, and the Attica riot, and about the justice system. And I knew my friend was still pushing me to realize some truths about prison.

I began to read and understand more, and I made a connection between the Attica riot and the racism inherent in my own war—the Long Bình Jail (LBJ) uprising, where the military prison was overcrowded. A straightforward article by Sarah Kramer tells it all: "Originally built to house 400 inmates, in August of 1968, LBJ was crammed with 719 men. And—in a mirror of the U.S. justice system—Black soldiers were greatly overrepresented in the jail. Despite representing 11% of the troops in Vietnam, more than 50% of the men incarcerated at the stockade were Black. Many Black soldiers felt they were more severely punished than white soldiers for similar offenses." (Sarah Kramer, NPR, August 28, 2018)

For me, LBJ was a harbinger of Attica. Most of the men in the jail were enlisted men—usually they'd faced a court-martial and been reduced in rank to private or private first class. There were no officers there. They didn't evaluate inmates for PTSD. There was no such thing in those years. The LBJ riot echoed the other very deliberate acts of racism I'd witnessed during my time in Vietnam. It is no coincidence that Nelson Rockefeller ordered the retaking of Attica prison after four days and nights of negotiations. No coincidence that then-President Nixon gave Rockefeller the "nod" on retaking the prison, no coincidence Nixon said, "It was a Black thing" and "The Angela Davis crowd needed to learn a lesson." The bloodiest and deadliest prison riot in American history. Three thousand rounds of ammunition used by NYS troopers and prison guards. September 13, 1971, in the rain.

The books the men in my class asked me to borrow and bring in for reading I read too. Of course, I had already read Malcolm X and Frederick Douglass, Harriet Jacobs and Angela Davis. Gradually,

48. Winter in America

books like *Blood in My Eye* by George Jackson, *The Blackstone Rangers* by Roger Sale, *Sex and Race* by J.A. Rogers and so many others began to fill my own personal library. In fact, before my time at Attica came to an end, I had met (brought into my class in person) Sonia Sanchez, Felipe Luciano, Don Lee/Haki Madhubuti, and Nancy Dupree, and I had read many more Black writers as well as Tom Wicker's *A Time to Die* and the *NYS Commissioner's Report on Attica*. And in a very real way, I felt I had begun to be re-educated. Equally important, I began to realize the kinship I felt for the men in my class was genuine. And I realized if slavery had continued by "another name" during Reconstruction and beyond, the prison "slave system" was all too evident in the years after the Attica uprising, even as the authorities tried to accommodate new "programs" and the like. Although I was free to leave each time our workshop ended, I felt tied to the men I met there, and I felt I had begun to understand a few *truths* about America.

And although this all happened many years ago, I never really left Attica—or Attica has never really let go of me—but except for a poem or two, I have been unable to write about my impressions of what it was like teaching a workshop there in the years immediately after the riot.

And then in 2010, nearly 34 years after my first summer in Attica, I read Michelle Alexander's *The New Jim Crow, Mass Incarceration in the Age of Colorblindness*.

It hit home. It made me realize I wasn't crazy and that my anger and frustration at what I had witnessed there in the late 1970s was grounded in *truth*, and it was okay to write about it, it was in fact good to be able to tell the truth about my feelings and my observations. I began a second "wake-up call" as the men in my class would have called it, but I still had this nagging reluctance to write about how I'd felt and what it had been like, what I had observed going inside. In 2015, I read Tom Robbins' article in the *New York Times* and felt another tug at my sleeve. And I emailed Mr. Robbins to ask what he thought about trying to write about those days in the 1970s.*

---

* https://www.nytimes.com/2015/03/01/nyregion/attica-prison-infamous-for-blood shed-faces-a-reckoning-as-guards-go-on-trial.htmlhen.

Part VII—Falling Forward

Finally, in 2016 I read *Blood in the Water* by Heather Ann Thompson, and I knew the anger and frustration I still felt all these years later was not unjustified or crazy but part of my own awakening, part of what it meant for me to be an American, and I needed to write about my own recollections and reflections—not as an historian or a sociologist or a journalist, but as a young man who came to realize many truths about our country inside the prison; truths that we still cannot face about racism and the footprints it leaves on all of our policies and programs; the tattoo we cannot remove or erase. It is imperative, even essential for white folks to respond to what they know to be true about the American "justice" system, and the police and the prejudice and racial hatred inherent in even the simplest acts.

Suddenly, I felt as if a heavy coat had been lifted a wet, dark raincoat like the one I used to wear when I taught at Attica; a size 20 raincoat my parents had bought me in high school, and one that I wore to Attica for most of the time when the weather was bad or snowy—or in other words, most of the time. Thompson's book makes it perfectly clear that what I had experienced in Attica in the years after the riot, what I felt and what I learned and what I read and dreamt about was *real*. In fact, the truths I learned at Attica—about myself, about my country, about prison and our justice system—had all been suddenly validated. On purpose. That's it really: "If you are here on purpose, you will come back on purpose."

The voices of those men I met there stay with me. I grew to love their refusal to succumb to Attica; their voices full of both anger and regret; and more importantly, a quiet resistance. As some of the men might jokingly note: *Time stamp: Now.*

And all at once the world of those prison days and nights came back in so many flashes of memory, quips of conversations, guys reading their poems and stories, cigarette smoke and the scrape of chairs pushed back.

I knew most of the men in my class were men who had been hit with drug charges—marijuana and cocaine. Others had two or three busts for theft and ended up doing 25 years to life. Still others had "copped" a plea and taken hard time. And then there were the guys

48. Winter in America

who had violated parole and ended up doing more time upstate at Attica.

~ ~ ~

The last Saturday morning I was there, I walked out through the tunnels that led to the different blocks and to "Times Square" as they called the central place where all the alleys came together, walking with the men who had come to the workshop. The guards frowned on walking with inmates, but we were the only class in the school on Saturdays, so I always walked out with the men. That morning, Mustapha—who had been in the riot in 1971—was one of the last to leave the line as we walked toward the front gate. He told me to look up at the plastic wood they had used to cover up the bullet holes in the wooden beams. "You need to see what's around you." And he said quietly, "Don't lose your sense of discovery—your willingness to keep asking questions." Good advice, even now all these years later.

And I knew he was pushing me to remember where I was and what had happened here. Mustapha always wore the same knit cap he'd worn during the uprising, and I remember how he smiled at me as he turned off to go to his block. "Be careful," he said. What the men in my class gave me is a kind of clarity, a clarity about observing things as they are, a way to learn to look closely at the things around you.

Now I believe when I drove back from Attica to the different towns where I lived then—first a cottage near Lakeville, New York, and later a big house I shared with some college students in Perry, New York (which was a much shorter drive)—I began to understand more about prison and about the lives of the men who were in prison.

My first summer there was a wake-up call for me, a white boy from upstate New York, who had never met a Black person until Parris Island and the Marine Corps. I make no apologies about my naiveté even after my tour in Vietnam, but perhaps ignorance gave me a special window—call it my (wood) *chuck* view. Attica stays with me, even after all these years. Gil Scott-Heron knew—and listening to his song "The Prisoner" brings me into the head again, as if I were

Part VII—Falling Forward

still there, going back and forth on those back roads, smoking cigarettes, angry and alone. And nothing to do but keep on.

The notions I had about race and class were vague and unfocused. Attica brought all the things I had read about and heard about into focus. It may be difficult for some to understand the kinship I felt with the men in my workshop, but for the first time since I had returned from Vietnam, I felt I had really come *home.* I think home is as much a place as it is a feeling. And in Attica I felt as if I were home; the home my Black friend Ward had warned me about on those rainy monsoon nights in Anton, near Chu Lai in 1966.

~ ~ ~

In Attica prison I met men who had fought in Vietnam, and their candor about their own homecomings made me see that my feelings of alienation, even exile, were in fact, real. Even if I had not gone to state prison, even if I were not Black or Latino, the *world* (the word veterans used to call home) I knew was different than the world the men in my class inhabited, but we shared a connection. Call it a *class consciousness,* and my feelings of kinship arose in part out of a shared set of *some* experiences, and, more importantly, out of not having to lie about what had happened to me (or us) after the war. The men in my class gave me that feeling of kinship. They acknowledged me and I still thank them for that acknowledgment. It was an acknowledgment born out of respect for each other.

As the class grew, I asked the Office of Volunteer Services and Hospital Audiences Incorporated (who was giving me a small stipend for the class) if I could add one day a week to my schedule. I began going in on Saturday mornings and Wednesday evenings—and the group started to come together.

~ ~ ~

I remember the callout sheets with the men's names and numbers; that's how you knew who was in the class and who would be coming that session. And I remember the vocabulary, the words that are unique to prison and the words I still use to show frustration and helplessness.

48. Winter in America

off the count—meaning a man didn't show that night or day, and the other secondary meaning—not there, away/gone.

keep-lock, the box, solitary, the hole, isolation—all terms for keeping a man away from others.

bid (I did three years), *my bid*—not a real bid, but the way the men told it, my bid.

slow down—guard tactic to stop a special visitor or program from happening, or just to stop anything a guard/hack wanted to stop or slow down.

lifer—meaning someone who was up for a long time.

chuck—meaning white dude and short for woodchuck, meaning me.

block—a section of cells in the prison, B block, A block, C block, D block—the block where the riot started.

stick, club baton, pole, billy club, ax—usually a wooden stick used by the guards.

co, hack, police—correction officer and different terms for jailers/guards.

cracker—white guy, usually anti–Black, anti–Latino, anti-liberal.

jailhouse joint—a thin marijuana cigarette (usually with too little THC to really be illegal and usually supplied by guards for a good price).

jail—another term for prison.

There were many other kinds of terms; check out Ted Conover's fine *New Jack* for more recent words and phrases.

Looking back, one song keeps surfacing, a song from my first year there. It's a song that haunts the other years, too—"Winter in America" by Gil Scott-Heron and Brian Jackson from their album called *First Minute of a New Day*. For me, this song works on several levels. Winter was Attica's season. If you could get there in the winter, you would know those roads and the snow that drifted across them. After the September rains and October's cool, crisp days, winter took over. My first winter there it snowed from mid–November straight through January; it snowed almost every day.

You had to drive through the snow to get there, and you had to drive *back* through the snow. I remember how it was to drive those

Part VII—Falling Forward

back roads in the snow after my class at night, my car pulling left then right. In those days I drove an old Dodge Dart with a slant-six engine; a car that had been yellow and we'd hand-painted (with brushes) a deep red with gel-oil house paint. It had wide oval tires on the rear—no snow tires—and it had a home-installed stick shift because the column shifter had broken off. The doors didn't lock and were held in by bungee cords. It was a good car in the snow—low to the ground yet easy to maneuver, and it would buck through the drifts like a large sled with wheels.

Winter was also the time to see the prison; a time to come upon it in the early winter dusk and realize how far it was from anywhere, how isolated it was, especially in the snow. You had to see the walls in the snow to know its isolation, to *feel* it. On those snowy days it felt like a prison out of the 19th century, an island of gray stretching over the frozen farmland.

~ ~ ~

I never wore a watch while teaching at Attica. I had thrown away my watch in 1967, and I had never owned one since. But Attica made you aware of time—there were so many ways to look at time. Time rules in prison. *Doing time, keeping time, marking time.*

Most of all, I remember the faces of the men I knew there—especially those men I came to know well, who came back to *our class* as they called it—the workshop we had in all kinds of weather. If I can say anything about them now, it will have to be about the way they saw me.

"We can smell freedom on you," one man told me. *"We can smell the outside."* I was a smoker then and I usually just tossed my cigarettes out on the table we sat around, so anyone who needed a smoke could have one. There was a resiliency in the men I came to know well. Mac, who was on his third bid and doing 25-to-life for his last robbery, wrote for the prison newspaper, sent out short poems for greeting cards, and was a reader. He loved plays. When I met him, he was in his fifties and had been inside most of his life. He had a deep, sonorous voice and a wisdom on all things about prison. During that first year he told me, "You know some of these guys are *cons* and they don't always tell you the truth."

48. Winter in America

I knew he was trying to help me out. Most of the men I knew in prison were Black or Puerto Rican. There were only four white guys who stayed in the class for any length of time.

And it's the faces of the men that still come back today, those faces and the stories they held—a raw, unforgiving fierceness of knowing how the system works and keeps you coming back to jail, back to the same traps, back to the sameness of days, back to the routines and the cold damp of cellblocks, back to solitary, darkness and lingering anger. And it's those men who stay with me: Mac, Willie D. Shea-Shea (aka Bobby R.), Ray C., Sonny, Doc, Ike, Hollywood, Ray P., Shakur—their names spin at me and I see them all again. Some nights in deep winter no one showed but a few men, and we'd sit around talking and reading what they had written until the school guards said we had to close it up. You can't forget the ties you make with men you know for two years or more, or even men you knew for a few months.

Their words stay with me: "They sing both tones of freedom" or "One and one and one make three—God got killed in Tennessee," and "Tomorrow belongs to those who prepare for it today" or so many other lines—read again and again until most of us knew those poems, and knew they rose up out of the same oppression and injustice.

In late August after almost three years teaching the workshop at Attica prison, I got a letter from the Superintendent's Office with a CC to the Office of Volunteer Services stating my privileges had been revoked. I'd written a letter to one of the men who had been in my class for over two years and who had been in "the box" for a couple of months. The administration had found the letter to be *out of line*. Writing had gotten me into teaching the class there, and I guess it was appropriate that writing also got me kicked out.

And I learned not to take words like *freedom* for granted, or other words too—words that help us to remember and recall who we are, how we came here, where we still might go. But we have to recognize ourselves in our Black counterparts, we have to see the things our own history insists on refusing to acknowledge and keeps tucked away from us, and we have to change—change seems

Part VII—Falling Forward

the hardest thing for so many of us—we have to feel *the need* to change.

I know you know those words of Frederick Douglass quoted so many times by so many are vital: "If there is no struggle, there is no progress.... Power concedes nothing without a demand. It never did and it never will." For me so is Douglass's statement about home and the need for a home from one of his last speeches, "Why the Negro is Lynched":

"Every man who thinks at all must know that home is the fountain head, the inspiration, the foundation and main support, not only of all social virtue but of all motives to human progress, and that no people can prosper, or amount to much, unless they have a home, or the hope of a home."

The Take-Away

To understand that for most men (and women) in prison, recidivism is in fact *"You're here on purpose and you will come back on purpose"* (as one well-known Black poet said), and this is the essential code of the prison system and of the racism inherent in that system. No *home* in the joint or in the street. Repeat: on purpose.

To realize that writing alone will not change anything—although this seems the antithesis of what a writer may believe—it is unfortunately a truth. Change will only come from action. Writing itself is a "kind of action," but it does not go far enough—something I only came to realize after I had left Attica. I could help those guys to write poems and personal narratives, but I could not help them find work when they got out of the joint; I had no connections to organizations or individuals who could help them stay out of prison. And my efforts were really in vain.

I write this now knowing there are many who believe writing by prisoners is and remains resistance narrative(s), and I do not argue—writing is resistance and a strong historical "push back" against oppression and injustice—but writing by prisoners alone will not change the prison system or the recidivism inherent in the system.

48. Winter in America

To realize my Attica time was self-education. In effect, I did learn many things that would prove useful when I got a chance to teach in literacy programs and eventually in college. Attica helped to shape my awareness. And it helped me to learn more about what I would not do and what I would not accept from my colleagues. It didn't help me to make many friends. I stayed angry and aware.

It may be many will see my personal narrative as naïve and fractured—to them I would say let me take you to one class, just one, on a snowy March night like the Wednesday night I brought Walt and a poet friend of his who had done time in prison for possession of drugs into the class. I'll drive the car, and after a two-hour session with the 10 men who were able show up out of the 20 who were on the list, we will leave and take those back roads back to an apartment at least a 40-minute drive depending on the road conditions and then sit there in a steamy kitchen and talk about what happened that night—who showed and who was locked down, and what the men were writing about.

There are no conclusions. As you knew and feared, anger can tear a person apart, and anger always brings despair and a lingering grief. Maybe this new generation of young people will change things. I don't think change comes without struggle and effort. And part of the change has to be in how men and women who have been in prison face the outside world again. They can't do it alone. They can't do it without a system that enables them to find meaningful work. I remember one of the men in my workshop who had done over eight years on a possession of cocaine charge. I remember him calling me when he made it back home, asking me if I could help him find work in the city school system where I was teaching writing to junior high and high school students through a Title I ESEA grant. I spoke to my supervisor. I spoke to her supervisor. No one could see their way into giving him a position as a security guard or hall monitor. It was "too risky," they said. "We can't take a chance." I knew he was disappointed, but I could not find him any meaningful work. I don't know what happened to him once my position ended in the spring. I had to find a job myself—and it was just part-time college teaching with part-time pay.

Part VII—Falling Forward

I keep remembering Miguel Hernandez's line from his poem "Train of the Wounded"—"There are no way stations for us, except in the hospital or else in the breast, on a single corner of flesh, you can put up a man."

Addenda: January 2022

1. All mail was censored. I discovered this one Saturday morning as I was leaving and I met a young man I knew from undergraduate school with a degree in sociology whose job at Attica was to read all inmate mail, not just for contraband, but for **the content** of the letters themselves.

2. Contraband—especially marijuana and drugs—were brought in by correction officers, aka *police*, aka *hacks*. A nice pay bonus for those locals who wanted to make extra cash.

3. Slow-downs and no shows to class were common. This was a technique to keep men from coming to class.

4. Transfers. Often men were transferred to another prison without notice. This meant the contents of the man's cell was often "tossed" or disposed of—books, papers, and the like. This happened to one of the men in my class—on Wednesday Willie was in class, and by Saturday he'd been transferred to Dannemora (nicknamed "Siberia") and a former hospital for the criminally insane, another maximum-security prison near the Canadian border now called Clinton Correctional Facility.

5. Visitors. On Saturday mornings I would see the Trailways buses, up from New York City and other points south. A five- or six-hour bus ride for a short hour or two visit—depending on the weather, depending on the guards, depending on circumstances. I'd get through the lines because of my workshop, but the visitors had to wait. They had to be checked and re-checked.

In the nearly three years directing the workshop at Attica, I supported myself by painting houses and working part-time jobs. I did not apply for any teaching positions in colleges or schools. All monies received from the publication of *Inside: Writing by Attica Inmates*, 1977, *Convicted Voices* by Lawrence Ike Dillard, and *Death Row* by James Fitzpatrick, were donated into the printing and publication of

48. Winter in America

Attica prison, summer 1978. Top row, left to right: unknown, Benny N., the author, unknown, unknown. Bottom row, left to right: Hollywood, Walter Shepperd and daughter, Howard W.

additional chapbooks. Many copies of the prison books were sent to anyone in prison—free of charge. My imprint for those chapbooks was La Huerta Press, a magazine and press that had some library subscriptions and was a not-for-profit endeavor.

49

(Who Wrote) The Book of Love?

It's noon on a Thursday in late May and I'm sitting in a hospital room/locked ward talking to a young man I've known since he was in nursery school. He's 19 and has a good shock of red hair and dark eyes—I'm watching his eyes as I try to talk to him. He has his father's good looks, his father's sharp-edged intelligence. I tell him Odysseus had red hair, you know, and it wasn't a wooden horse they used to get inside the gates of Troy but real cattle—they sewed themselves inside the cattle. The Trojans were hungry. You have that kind of cunning, that kind of smarts, that keen intelligence. I think he's listening. It's his dad's birthday and I tell him maybe that will give me an opening, maybe he'll listen. His father died in his arms. Mark held him while his mother called 911. But Mark was the one who held his own father. Cancer. His father was too far gone and he'd never told them. He was only 53.

I look at his wrists. He has red, chafed wrists from the handcuffs the police put on him to bring him in here. Red flashes from the tasers they hit him with on both shoulders. He was in a semi-coma for two days and he still is on a drip to help him get the stuff out of his system. His left hand is limp—nerve damage he thinks. Every few minutes someone comes in to ask about the food, has he gone to the bathroom, is he voiding?

I keep trying to get his attention, trying to turn the corner, get him thinking about other things. Things he might do. I try to tell him about my own baggage, the summer when I was 19, my mother's death when I was only four, my abusive stepmother, my father's anger. I try to tell him about folks who helped me turn a

49. *(Who Wrote) The Book of Love?*

corner, to quit getting "messed up" and to start doing something for myself.

I'm not sure he's buying it, but I know he's listening. I remember his father and I know how his father would feel about seeing his son dragged into a hospital room cut and bleeding and half gone with drugs. I think about what David would say, how he'd say it. Before David lost his job and then got sick and a little crazy, we were good friends. I liked his dad. There was a good kind of honesty about him. Our sons grew up together. I tell him straight out—your father would never go for this, Mark. He'd be angry about it. He'd want you to listen.

~ ~ ~

50

Pavane

She is a mother. She is and remains a mother even though her child dies. For at one time she carried the child under her heart. And it does not go out of her heart ever again.
Kore—an Ethiopian woman

You died as a result of medical incompetence and negligence. Even though I can never know the things your mother knew, I know what it felt like to hold you in my arms. I know what you looked like, how your head was shaped. I felt your weight in my arms. And I know what it is like to follow the ambulance from one hospital to the intensive care unit of another. I know the slow fear that came over me as I followed the lights of the highway at 3 a.m. I remember the snowdrifts like tufts of stone in the early light. I know the rooms they took you to, and I know the machines they plugged you into until eventually the machines alone kept you alive; the machines that made it seem we really had you with us when you had gone from us already. I know it was the machines and the doctors who worried about insurance companies, so they kept us coming back for 12 days until they let you go at last. We named you Luke before you were born, before the hospitals and the doctors.

Someday when your younger brothers ask who you were, I suppose I will have to tell them. I'll tell them you were born in February in the leap year, and I will go over it all again.

It is true I cannot know what it is to lie alone in a hospital bed waiting, after so many months of carrying you. I can never know what it is like not to have you at my breast and to feed you and comfort you as only a mother can do. Instead, what I know is the dark, the sense I could not make it right. This is my place.

50. Pavane

To know the way the undertaker was dressed the day I went to make the arrangements for your burial. I know the way his office looked—the white clapboard building in a grove of trees. I know the tiny coffin they put you in and the undertaker's cream-colored Subaru hatchback that came to the cemetery with your body.

And I know out of all the harm I've seen men do, the cruelties that pass for honor, duty, all the old lies—nothing prepared me for the way you entered this world. Your mother packed in ice, hurting so much I couldn't stop her tears.

Yesterday, playing football with your younger brothers in the street, watching the ball fly toward the oldest—the one who wouldn't be here if you had lived—I think I glimpse you as you might have been—12 years old and strong and quick already, with hair like your great-grandfather, and dark brown eyes, handsome and smart like your mother. And for a minute I cannot see the street or your brothers or time. I can see who you might have been and what we would be like if you had lived, where we might be now. *"Pass the ball,"* they yell at me, and the image of you is gone again. There is just the street and the bare branches of the trees, the cries of your brothers rising in play. I think of the hillside where we buried you in that cemetery where your great-grandmother lies, the copper beeches bare in the March grayness, and an old anger rises up in me. I can know anger. I can know that anger is just one of the stages of grief.

Eventually anger too lets go of us. But I see you in your brothers—those two who came after you. I see you in the youngest one who is 14 now, and at birth who weighed even more than you—almost 10 pounds—delivered naturally. Even the doctor stood back from his birth. Forgive me this. Forgive me seeing your high forehead in his high forehead—his dark eyebrows like yours might have been. His head seeming almost too big for his shoulders, and he reminds me of you.

Sometimes I find myself telling perfect strangers about what happened. I think they look at me quizzically, as if to ask why not let go of this? Yet, I have never been able to let go of even the small things, let alone you. All the arguments your mother and I had—the things we needed but could not afford, the tests she had to take to

Part VII—Falling Forward

make sure you were okay, the check-ups, the long drives back through snow country to our home, the friends who called to ask, "Hey, how are you guys?" The pictures we took of your mother—getting bigger, her hair so dark then—I still see her in denim overalls, six months pregnant and watching your grandfather and I build a grape arbor in the back yard.

And your mother has never forgiven me for not going to counseling afterward, for not trying to get the both of us in a group therapy session. She's still angry that I went back to work after two weeks. She remembers the call from my chairperson—the morning you died—after they pulled you off the machines that were keeping you alive. My chair wanted to know if I had completed the report on the writing program, a report she said she needed. I told her you had died that morning and we were going back to the hospital to make the necessary arrangements. She was insistent. I finally told her I would call her in a couple days.

~ ~ ~

51

Rivers of My Fathers

The river moves past the towns where I grew up; its name stays with me; its wandering course part of my life, *Susquehanna.* Even today its name still slides in all its syllables off my tongue, brings back my Uncle Baldo coming in the side porch door with a brown bag full of mushrooms he has picked in the damp woods above the river where Nanticoke Creek empties out.

After being laid off from the Buick plant in Flint, Michigan, my uncle came to live with us and take a job in the shoe factories. *"Piecework,"* he'd say, shrugging his shoulders. When he got home from work in the late afternoons, he would climb the foothills out of the valley to hunt for mushrooms. He'd walk until the houses below seemed far off, and sometimes he took me with him, showing me how to pick the ones that were good to eat. In the early spring and fall, he'd look for mushrooms.

The rivers of home had names that rose out of their estuaries in the tidewater country—first as Algonquian names, then later as Lenape names and finally the Iroquois names, too. The names of those rivers and their tributaries conjure up the ghosts of those who lived before the factories and farms—Susquehanna, Chemung, Chenango, Nanticoke, Otsego, Swatara. Their waters rise in the smoke of campfires, in the mist and damp rain leavening off over dark green water.

~ ~ ~

When I left Rome once in early November, the driver who took us from the car drop-off place to the air terminal was playing some music in his van. It was a jazz remix song and the singer kept

Part VII—Falling Forward

repeating the line, *"I've known rivers, and my soul has grown deep like the rivers, rivers, rivers."*

I asked Alexis, the driver, who the artist was and he showed me the liner to the MP3—the name Courtney Pine and the title *I've Known Rivers Remix*. I told him (he was English and African and spoke three languages), that the song had been adapted from an African American poet named Langston Hughes. *"It's from a poem called 'The Negro Speaks of Rivers,'"* I said. My sons were looking at me from the back seat. Alexis nodded. *"We've got some music,"* he said.

The song, the poem, the young man driving us back to get our plane home—made me think about the rivers I'd crossed and re-crossed, and the Susquehanna again, my own home and the anger there that had led me away. I wrote to Alexis after I got my own copy of Courtney Pine's *Remix*.

Flying back to New York and coming home to the East River my father had loved as a boy, and the Hudson River we lived close to now, made me think about what home really means. Maybe you must leave home to understand it; maybe time itself helps you to understand where you come from and why you went away.

~ ~ ~

My son Ben has forgotten the first time he saw the river Tiber in Rome; it was late fall and the chestnut leaves were dropping. He has forgotten that he wanted to stop and toss coins over the edge; it was the Ponte Sisto—a walking bridge—and he insisted we stop so he could make a few wishes. Now I want to remind him of this; he's older and he doesn't remember his fascination with bridges and fountains. I know he has memories of our many trips to Italy when he was young, but I suppose time has left only its traces: a glimpse of leaves falling, the night's dark growing as we walked across the river. I remember lifting him up so he could throw coins over the edge.

In the photograph all three of my sons stand on the covered bridge that Palladio designed and built along the River Brenta in Bassano del Grappa. The early fall rains have swelled the banks of the river behind them. They are smiling: Nick, the oldest, Ben and

51. Rivers of My Fathers

Nate—their backs to the water rushing behind them. We are on our way south again crossing the Adige, a river the poet James Wright loved—a river swollen with the recent rains—south toward Rome and our last few days in Italy. This has been our shortest trip—a little over a month. Rome again means we are close to leaving.

In Rome the starlings have already begun to swarm. It's the end of October. Michele and I remember those starlings from our earlier trips here, and from a book by Paul Hofmann called *The Seasons of Rome*. Hofmann writes, "They leave a carpet of guano on sidewalks and the street, cars (like ours) parked at curbsides overnight will be splattered all over." There is something special in these flocks of starlings and our walking again across the bridges across the Tiber: brings back our other visits, the first December we spent at the American Academy when we were all still young and our sons were young too.

Do our sons remember? It was chilly in Rome that first trip, and I am certain Nick remembers; he was 14 then. But Ben does not remember; he was only two years old and he loved fountains; we took him to every fountain in Rome. Now when I remind him of that trip and of the fountain of the turtles/La Fontana di la Tortugas in the Piazza Mattei, he shrugs it off. He's worried about the droppings from the starlings. Hofmann writes that ornithologists believe the starlings come from places in the north and "are particularly drawn to the Sabine Hills, roughly fifty miles east of Rome. There the birds devour insects, showing a particular liking for a kind of fly that infests olive trees with its larvae, thus the guests do useful pest control five days a week, rain or shine."

It seems like a good sign that the starlings are here with us again, swirling above the chestnut trees that line both sides of the river. On this trip the warm weather in Rome feels good after so much rain up in the north and it's good to walk in the places where we used to walk before.

This day, our Roman friend Luisa wants to take us to the Via Appia Antica to look for Seneca's tomb, but for one reason or another we go too far and instead end up at a villa belonging to the actress Gina Lollobrigida. Seneca will have to wait. It doesn't matter, walking

Part VII—Falling Forward

the road itself is a special thing—the huge stones worn smooth by time.

On the very first trip we took to Italy, my two younger sons were not yet born, and it was just Michele and Nick and me. On that trip I remember the bridge over the Arno in Firenze and how one early June evening in a drizzling rain we bought two small 5 × 7 watercolors, and now when I look at them on the landing of our home, that very evening comes back; the stray yellow dog we saw running along the edge of the river wall after we had crossed, the hunched-up old man walking behind the dog, the gathering dusk, the distant sounds of traffic. I see Nicholas in that light; how young he was, and his own watercolors, his own way of seeing where we were.

Of course, it was the Ponte Vecchio and it was the first crossing—our first time in Florence and we did the things tourists do. The next afternoon after driving out of the city, we had arranged to stay for a few nights at a small working farm where they let rooms with a small kitchen. Outside the woman who ran the place brought us a dish of strawberries and two glass pitchers—one we thought was strawberry juice and the other white wine. Nick and I poured ourselves glasses and began to eat the strawberries.

When Michele came down from the upstairs room, she poured a glass of white wine. Nick started to laugh. *"Hey you guys,"* he said. *"This one is wine, too."* And all three of us started laughing out there in the sunlight of that June day under the shade of the shrub oaks on that Tuscan farm.

~ ~ ~

Leaving Rome is difficult; it's like the small pieces of bread you use to dip into what's left of your pasta sauce—*scarpetti,* our friend Sergio calls them, "little shoes." We walk away with glimpses of our memories: the Caravaggios in the French Church, an alleyway near the Pantheon, the stark, dry fields of the Roman countryside, a late dinner in a trattoria off the Via Ripetta, the mercato on Sunday at the Porta Portese not far from the Protestant Cemetery, walking along the Tiber under the chestnut trees on a late fall day.

~ ~ ~

51. Rivers of My Fathers

When I think of my son Nate, I see the road leading to Chimney Mountain in the Adirondacks. I see Nate fishing from the rowboat on the King's Flow. There's a short wooden bridge where the water goes over into the stream below, and I remember how much he loved going up on that bridge, casting off into the pool below the waterfall. One afternoon when we were together out on the water, he said, "Look, the clouds are in the lake." I see him running toward me over that wooden bridge on a late August afternoon.

~ ~ ~

All three of our sons used to live near the East River. When they come home, my youngest son Nate says, *"It's too quiet up here."* Michele and I live above the Hudson—you can see it in the distance. We have a house that was once part of Hilltop Farm. Below our house there's an old dairy barn that has been converted into a home where our neighbor Andrew lives. All that is left of the farm is surrounded by center-entrance colonials and remodeled suburban ranch houses; Hook Mountain; the lower Hudson River; 10 miles to Manhattan. When Michele and I moved from upstate New York, our first apartment was in the old servant quarters in a mansion that had views of the Hudson River from the east windows.

When they all lived in Queens, my sons had to cross and re-cross the rivers of New York City every day. I wonder if they thought about those rivers, about crossings and returns. Maybe for them the rivers they have come to know—especially the East River, the Hudson, Arthur Kill, Richmond Creek, and the Flushing River—all seem to lead toward the ocean. I think there's something to this—to their need for travel, for searching, for learning how not to look back.

Maybe they each will find their own rivers in distant countries far from where they were born. *"I dream of journeys repeatedly,"* Theodore Roethke wrote in his poem "The Far Field." I think each of our sons has his own journey to make, his own crossing. And I know I have learned to see each one as a distinct person. Sometimes it's an effort to remind myself of this. I have to see them as separate individuals alone or together. I know there are rivers behind us—water shining in the sunlit mornings, water moving

Part VII—Falling Forward

and rushing past—but it's the rivers ahead of them I think of as well—the rivers they will cross, the bridges each one of them will take. And now that they are older, I know they will never be asked to serve in a war.

~ ~ ~

52

When I'm Gone

    Listen, the world keeps changing and sometimes what comes back is hard to face, like going out into a hailstorm and the hail is coming down, pelting you, making you look for cover and there is no cover. It's like that now when I see those faces or I start down some long hallway and lose track of where I am and what I'm doing and the hallway starts to tilt and go away from me, you know? That's when I start flipping into displacement 101. It's like the original dream, the one I keep seeing on playback—a profusion of detail, too much detail to comprehend, too much to understand. I see the dark corners come back. Yes, I know I should let some things go—let the memories slip out, ooze away.

    And sometimes I look for the face of someone I knew—is it Marshall from my first duty station in North Carolina? Marshall who said he'd probably stay in the Corps, it was easier than facing the world. He was from the Bronx. But it's been too long and I'm just one of the old guys myself now, hunched into my age and trying to shake it loose. No one gets it, how close the past seems and yet how far away. Or is it that I am searching for the boy I was then, what I might have become, and stumbling in the dying light, I think he's there—the boy and the man he might have become—as if he were driving the car ahead of me and doing the things I might have done without making all the mistakes, without falling down and forgetting. Maybe it's more than that, it's a dream I keep having about fighting off the hard edges of things—someone trying to smother me, suffocate me, stop me from getting up. Like a hand on my chest pushing me down. Once, my old internist told me at my annual physical that I had a bone in my chest, like a breast plate—he called it a sword—and then

Part VII—Falling Forward

I remember how my grandfather chose my name because it meant *spear wielder*.

The ghosts come back at night or sometimes even at midday—I see their signs, their leavings. I hear the wind picking up—like an inland sea, one poet called it—and I listen to the wind in the branches of the oaks, pulling though the boughs of the Norway spruce. I hear the wind coming close, pulling at me to keep remembering.

I want to meet up with him, this other man, this driver. I want to talk with him like I talked with Ward and Turner, like I talked with the men I knew at Attica, like the old men I met on the road crew in Iowa, as if I could have a new kind of conversation. And I remember a young teacher I had in high school who tried to get me to understand what I was too hard-headed to understand then—she said the choice was mine to make, but I had other choices.

The hail changes to rain and the rain keeps on. I hear it on the roof and in the leaves of the oaks; the street is glistening with the rain. And then there are those two mourning doves outside on the top of the arbor, singing their soulful song.

~ ~ ~

Epilogue: Collateral Damage

Orange Crush

Listen Bo, Chuck tells me about his wife's team in the Iraq War, you know the 2nd Iraq war, the one we fought over weapons of mass destruction—if you want to call it that—Operation Iraqi Freedom. I know Chuck kind of likes me because I'm an ex-jarhead from 'Nam, and I helped him with the PTSD review—his five-year checkup. I told him there were new criteria; it's the list my own doc gave me. Chuck works for the DPW; he's the crew chief, and he's a good guy.

You have to know there was strange stuff going on there, weird things, chemical agents, toxic blowouts. But this one beats it. You know the waterboarding, the crazy street fights, the RPGs, the children getting caught up in things that make you remember, reflect on your own past. Y'know? Things change, but then nothing changes. And then there are just the stories that come back. He says his wife was in the military too, part of a special ops team of women, and she's the only one left. The last one. Her team members are all dead.

Yellowcake—depleted uranium—left over in bomb craters, left over from the weapons we used, the bombs, and the special explosives, the aerial stuff that was dropped and dispersed. Suppose you slept in one of those craters with your team? Suppose you spent a couple of nights there? Holed up, waiting. You know, it's like that what we don't know about, what they don't want us to know about. Like my friend Frankie who has the shakes now at 76 years old; I mean, he can't stop shaking, so they just give him some pills and a check for $25 grand. A payoff. Called it exposure to chemical weapons. They don't even know. But they do know it causes organ damage. They know you can't shake it. You can't wash it off.

It's the same kind of deal with Chuck's wife. He says they took out all her female organs to get rid of the cancer. I'm afraid to ask him how she is doing when I stop to talk with him. I'm afraid about what he's going to tell me about what is happening. He says if it wasn't for some doctors in New York City, civilian docs, well the VA would've taken away her disability rating. No money for being so sick, for being on the edge.

Think about what she remembers, huh? You know there were two Iraq wars—those people who remained have the world's highest rate of lymphoma, that's what the WHO says, the highest rate of leukemia too. Check it out. All those places we've been are getting the dose. You know, the fallout. It lingers. You can read about it if you want to, but talking to Chuck on a fine day in late September is enough to give you a chill, it creeps over the landscape—the late summer boneset spreading out over the meadow the DPW crew has been restoring. And seeing those blossoms you can't shake what Chuck tells us again, repeating the story now with even more details.

And it's getting dark earlier, the days slipping away from us.

~ ~ ~

Can't Take My Eyes Off You

My friend Mark emails me about how he has just watched *The Deer Hunter* for the first time and he likes the scenes in the mountains in Pennsylvania—the depiction of the working-class men who fought in Vietnam—but instead I start to think of my next-door neighbors who used to bring home a deer in November and hang it up in their garage to gut and cut up in pieces for freezing. One fall day my friend Mike and I looked inside when Jimmy had left the door open, and we saw the newly shot deer hanging there with its legs tied

Collateral Damage

up to the rafters. We saw its antlers and then the other antlers hanging from the far wall.

And I remember again the night my friend Doris called and asked me to come right over to her home. She said in the high, nervous voice she had:

"Ger, you've got to come over to our house. You have to talk to Robert about what happened. You know. You've been there. You've seen things."

The day before a story in the newspaper was about a young 17-year-old high school junior who had shot himself in front of his two 16- and 15-year-old friends. He was playing the "Russian roulette scene" from *The Deer Hunter* using his father's gun, a .38 caliber pistol his father, a prominent lawyer, had hidden under the front seat of his car in case he needed protection in a criminal case. The boys had been watching the movie and decided to play the game.

Doris's son Robert (almost 17) was sitting next to his friend Michael when it happened. He'd been spattered with his friend's blood. Michael was Stewart's best friend.

I told Doris I'd drive over to her home, a restored Victorian in an exclusive suburb. I knew Doris from the Title 1 ESEA writing program I'd initiated and developed for the inner-city schools. Doris knew I was a Vietnam veteran, and she felt I could help her son understand and cope with the shooting. I tried to tell her I'd seen a lot of things, but I had never seen a friend accidently kill himself in the family room of his parents' home. I'd never seen anyone kill himself except on the neuro-psychiatric ward they sent me to after my own return from Vietnam. And that wasn't with a pistol, so I had time to think it over on the drive to her home.

When I got there, her husband was washing the dinner dishes in the kitchen and Doris and her son Robert were at the table in the dining room. Her husband Donaldson, also a lawyer and a Yale graduate, offered a glib hello and thanked me for coming over.

I didn't know what to say to his son. And I wish his parents had sat down with me at the table. Instead, the father started to dry the dishes, listening, and his wife Doris went into the living room.

I had only met Robert once or twice when I had stopped by their

Epilogue

home to drop off a contract or pick up some paperwork. He asked me about my war, about what I'd done there. And I tried to talk to him, tried to tell him that I had never seen a friend kill himself. I had never played roulette with a handgun, and I told him about my outfits, where I'd been.

I tried to ask him about the movie, about why they had started to play the game; a game that had already triggered over 35 copycat shootings—most of them critical. I tried to talk about the film, about how the character DeNiro had portrayed was really a character with traits similar to John Wayne—someone who wanted to be in the military, who found a kind of enjoyment in what he was doing. He had signed on for more years after he came back from the war, and he wasn't someone who had learned much of anything from what he had experienced, about what the film shows us about the war they'd fought. In fact, the Vietnamese were portrayed as the other—"evil killers" who also enjoyed *the game*. I guess I knew what Cimino was trying to suggest about the war there and about American involvement, but I didn't like the film.

Now for Robert, it was no game. It was just something he'd carry for the rest of his life. And I couldn't help him, and I'm not sure what his parents wanted from me. A Marine vet to talk with their son? Someone who had "been there" and come home? They'd also wanted my friend Frank who'd been in the Army near the DMZ to come over as well, but he wasn't around that night, and I had no way to get in touch with him. I wish Frank had come with me. It might have helped me to frame a kind of conversation with Robert.

I wish his parents had tried to sit with us, too. I wish they'd helped me to help their son.

But they didn't. Maybe that's what they wanted, for me to talk with Robert by myself.

An hour and a half later, I left. There was a kind of hole that talking with him left in me—he had given me the details, the Friday night when it had happened. The circle of five friends sitting in the family room after watching the film, drinking a few beers. One of the boys just 14. I have never shaken it off, never forgotten Robert or his questions or his parents, never forgotten the coolness of the late fall night, how it felt to drive back to my apartment on the other side of the city and how the dark kept pulling in at me, all the hard anger brewing up again, reminding me of the hurt and loss and now this kid with his friend dead and nowhere to go with it, nothing to do.

~ ~ ~

Eight Miles High

I think it started as a way to kick the stelazine the docs had given me when I left the hospital—enough stelazine for six months of sleep. But I didn't want to sleep, I didn't want to sleep it off, forget stuff, doze; and still I took it with me to college. Why? A cushion? A way to hold on. I had weaned myself off it by the last week in October. I knew it was a crutch, a link to the hospital and to coming home, a link to forgetting about Bernadette and Marie—old girlfriends whom I'd left back home as well. I felt the bottle of pills was a good thing, a way to connect the two parts of me, the old and the new. I never threw it away until my Black friend Howard tried to OD on 10 capsules after he got his midterm grades during our freshman year. And this pot thing started and I couldn't shake it. Twenty years asleep like Rip Van. Twenty years lost and uncounted.

Now Dr. Morley tells me stelazine is also a drug that changes your body chemistry and often makes one jittery and on edge. In my case it did both—I gained weight in spite of daily exercise, and I could not stop the on-edge feeling, the tipping-over sense of things. I often broke up my sentences, could not keep them from fragmenting and seeming to fly away. And this lasted for months since I did not stop taking the pills until the night Howie flipped out. Now I know why it was so easy to pick up smoking pot—easy to get a cushion against reality—especially easy to start each day by blowing some smoke and drinking cups of coffee. A whole new way of looking at the day.

~ ~ ~

Epilogue

Sam Stone

Dom Rep

Listen, Bo. Now another winter drums its way into the days and nights. And I keep seeing things, you know, remembering. My wife shakes me in the dark and asks, "Who are you talking to? Why are you so restless?"

I can't tell her the truth. I can't tell her I'm thinking about the night those motor-pool sergeants got drunk, and Sgt. Drake—well, he got crazy and started to scream about what had happened to him and his outfit down in Dom Rep. I was a few months into being 19 then and didn't know what Dom Rep was or why the Marines and the Army had been there. No one liked Sgt. Drake; he was a burly, six-foot s.o.b. with his short, blond hair almost white from the sun or early aging. He always talked to you as if you were not there. He was nearly 30, which was old to us. And he spoke to most of us who were still PFCs or lance corporals with disdain.

That one night he couldn't let go of it, and now I still remember his screams. They were so loud; we heard him down in our tents. Finally, Sgt. Forster called for Doc Thomas, the corpsman, who heard the crazy screaming and was going up there anyway. Doc must have hit him with something to quiet him down, to get him to sleep it off. But it took a good while and I can still hear the sarge yelling about the street fights, how they hid behind dumpsters ... burned out cars, trucks. And the wounded, how many men they'd lost. That's what he was screaming about. The guys who were wounded, over 140 men. "For what?" he screamed. "For fucking what?"

"We shot dogs, we shot up the streets, we shot anything and everything that moved."

In the morning Doc Thomas told me about Sgt. Drake and about what he'd been through, and I felt like I knew more about why he spoke to us like he did—as if we were not there, as if he couldn't see us—it was a kind of safety net, a screen.

Now, I know Dom Rep was the Dominican Republic and that President Johnson had sent in close to 40,000 troops—both Marines and Army—to suppress the newly elected president of the country, a man Johnson had mistakenly been advised was a communist-leaning official. Johnson believed it would become another Vietnam—a place he felt had taken over his current presidency—it was mid-winter 1967 and LBJ had begun to feel the weight of his own albatross.

Back then I didn't know what the sarge had been through, how bad it had been and how much he had seen and lived through only to find himself in Vietnam less than a year later. It must have made him crazy. And then we were nine months short of the first Tet Offensive. Did the sarge move with our outfit into Hue? Did he see it all happen again? I went home in early July. But a lot of the men still had time to serve, enough to catch it at Hue City when the battalion moved up there.

~ ~ ~

If I Could Only Fly

You know I'd never been to jail before that county jail in Syracuse. I'd never been handcuffed before either. Now, my wife Michele asks me why I iron the bed sheets and pillowcases, why it's important. And I tell her because in jail you didn't get sheets or pillows, and I remember this, like I remember how it was back then—the first jail and then the Brooklyn Brig and the way it was down there in Brooklyn. How you went to chapel on Sunday to get out of the block, to get some freedom away from the tiers of bunks and cells. The brig was better than jail in some ways. You could smoke all the time. And there were no cells, just the open block. The small holding cell they brought me to at the Marine Barracks at Portsmouth was different. There were only three cells. And just two were occupied—mine and the one next to mine. It was a solitary lock-up. No walkaround. No anything. The guy next to me was a runaway who was going south to Camp Lejeune. I was going to the real brig in Portsmouth. And for the night, they kept me there.

The other civilian jails I found myself in all happened after my discharge, after the months on the locked NPS ward. The first jail

Epilogue

after my discharge was a "mom and pop" jail in Susquehanna, Pennsylvania. I'd been out of the Marines for less than two months and got busted in Pennsylvania with some friends. We'd been cruising around in Carmine's car and it was late and the cops pulled us over. I was the oldest at 20—and the Pennsylvania State Police got my records and saw I'd been arrested before for the stuff that had happened my second night back from Vietnam—so they held me overnight in that jail in Susquehanna until my parents came down the next morning and paid my $50 fine and got me out. The other guys, all under the age of 18, the police let them go back home to Endicott, New York. My parents weren't too happy about the bust or the fine.

The next jail was in my first year of college. And as my friend Mr. Vonnegut would say—"So it goes."

This was a stupid bust. My housemate Howie, who worked as a bartender at The Variety Inn, well, he'd given a guy a ride home to crash on our couch. Howie really didn't know who the dude was or where he'd been. I found that out when we got busted for something we didn't do: steal money from an "automatic pay" gas pump near the college. The guy who was riding around with me—call him George—he was AWOL from the Army. None of us knew anything about him, but he didn't get out of jail with me. He had to be sent somewhere to face the military charges. I don't know what happened to him.

While I was teaching at Attica, I used a grant I had from Poets & Writers and The NYS Council on the Arts to visit county jails and conduct writing workshops with prisoners. I got to visit some of the more isolated jails, and sometimes I took a musician with me, a guy who was versatile on the guitar and banjo, just to connect with those boys, since most of them were just that—boys, and usually under 20, too—doing up to a year in the county jail for whatever they'd done.

~ ~ ~

Nature Boy

When my father told me my stepmother had walked off into the sprinklers on the yard of Uncle John and Aunt Grace's home in Tom's River, we were driving in my father's car along the Delaware River. And instead of thinking about Alzheimer's and my stepmother, I remembered the time my Uncle Pete—who was married to my stepmother's sister Angie—came into our upstairs bathroom one night after I had taken a bath and was about to go to bed and showed me a small match box toy with a boy outside on an island—when you opened the matchbox the boy began masturbating. I was a ten year old boy then. That day riding with my father in his car and listening to him tell how he knew he had to get help for my stepmother, I asked him about Uncle Pete. And then, quite honestly, my father said:

"Well, you know Uncle Pete was a pedophile, don't you? You know everyone knew he was not all right."

And that was the first time my father ever mentioned Uncle Pete's issue. And he did it as if I should have known, as if I could. I remember how my Uncle Pete tried to follow me into my bedroom that night and how I just wanted to be free of him. When he turned to go back downstairs, he didn't say anything.

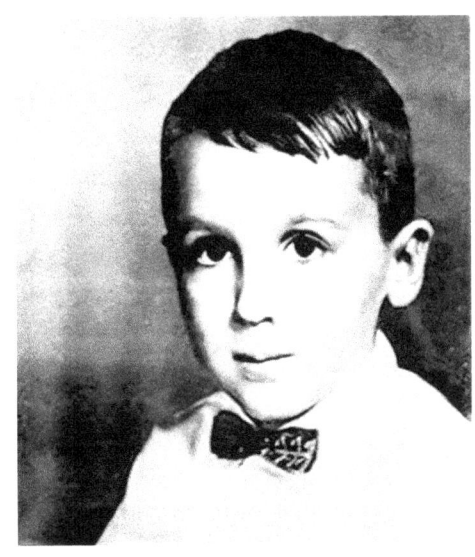

The author, seven years old, not an innocent young boy any longer (photograph by William McCarthy).

~ ~ ~

Epilogue

The Runaway

It's there in the basement. A nylon rope long enough to tie to a beam and make the leap. Doc calls it ideation and it's ok to have some ideation. But I have not told the doctor about it. I have not told him much of the truth. Usually, in our sessions, I try to stay on the positive. And I think he likes that I do, but I'm not being honest with him. I'm leading him on, letting hm think I'm okay. And I keep saying to him if I get at the truth, I'll be better. But that's not the case. In fact, the more I remember, the worse it gets.

Hard to explain this. Hard to stick to the topic. Why checkout? Where does that leave you? But at times it rises up like bile, like a hard crisp edge you can't climb over—a gulf you can't cross. Not to make a big deal about it. As long as it's there, well, maybe it serves as a safety net. A thing with its own life, its own persona.

~ ~ ~

Time Has Come Today

So just as I think I'm done writing this and like I'm letting go of it, the artist Jane Irish sends me a catalog from her new exhibit. Before I've even had a chance to see some of the new work she has completed, I turn to one of the last pages and an image of the Winter Soldier Investigation Testimony comes up—an excerpt about the stoning of a three-year-old child. And then I read again Bill Hatton's testimony, his explanation.

> "Hatton: my duty was to go out and serve as a perimeter guard on the Dong Ha ramp."
> This was an LCU ramp on the Quat River where Navy ships came up and they'd off-load supplies. We took our truck outside the combat base every night at 5:30 to set up at the ramp for our night's duty. We used to drive by this row of hootches and a little three-year-old kid in dirty grey shorts used to run out and scream, "You, Marines number 10," and we'd always go back, "Oh, you kid" and all this stuff. So, one night the kid comes out and says, "Marines, you Number 10" and throws a rock. So, we figured we'd get him because this was a way of having fun. The next night before we went out, we

all stopped by COC, which is right by the ammo dump, picked up the biggest rocks we could get our hands on and piled them in the back of the truck. So, when we left the combat base, we just turned the corner and we saw a little kid, we were waiting for the kid—he ran out of the hootch—and he was going to scream "Marine Number 10" and we didn't even let him get it out of his mouth. We just picked up all the rocks and smeared him. We just wiped him out. In fact, the force of the rocks was enough to knock over his little tin hootch as well. I can't say that the kid died, but if it would have been me, I would have died easily. The rocks, some of them, were easily as big as his head. It was looked upon as funny. We all laughed about it. It took me about a year to even be able to recall the situation. I think it said something about the entire attitude of us over there. I never had a specific hatred for the Vietnamese, I just tended to ignore them. They didn't figure in any calculations as to being human. "They either got in the way or they weren't there."*

~ ~ ~

You Made Me So Very Happy

Blood and guts. That's what the assistant head coach called it. It was two big linemen vs. one lineman. In this case the lineman was a guard with quarterback shoulder pads—no protection since they were too small. I weighed 155. The two linemen in the faceoff with me weighed over 200 lbs. each, thus the title of the exercise. I had the guts; they were out for blood. Usually, I gave it three tries before the coach blew the whistle on my turn. By then those guys had knocked me down all three times. No big deal, I survived. My shoulder pads didn't help, and it made it easier to manhandle me. I don't know why they made me a defensive guard; weird, since there were other bigger players on the team. I played for 10 minutes in five or six games. Once I was lucky enough to recover a fumble. That was my whole year of junior varsity football. In my junior and senior years, I went out for cross-country.

---

* Jane Irish, New Catalog, February 2021/Locks Gallery, Philadelphia, Pennsylvania. The testimony is from *The Winter Soldier Investigation–An Inquiry into American War Crimes, Vietnam Veterans Against the War*, Beacon Press, Boston, 1972. pp. 69–70 (Cpl. William Hatton, 3rd Marine Division).

Epilogue

You can't tell how things are until you get to the turning point, a place in your head where you can see things in relief, like you have perspective on your own past, like it matters. And the things that have happened take on a new significance. Now in those days, I had a girlfriend—and she was my friend, too—trying to educate me, trying to hip me to music, like quit listening to movie themes and The Beatles and check out Dave Brubeck, you know. "Take Five." I should have listened to her. She was older, in the class ahead of me in high school, and she was intelligent and kind. But it's like that stupid football exercise—I wasn't mean enough, tough enough, I wasn't paying attention to the details—it took me too long to get it and by then, I was in country and writing letters home.

Waltzing Matilda

I first met Mary "Edie" Meeks as part of a grant that I had to develop a series of programs on World War I and America for the Gilder Lehrman Center for American History, the National Endowment for the Humanities and the Library of America. It was the centennial of World War I and the grant's focus was on bringing American veterans into the audience for the events. I taught a course on World War I using film and novels. My focus for the public aspect of the course was to arrange a series of talks in a local library and our own college library that reflected all aspects of war and its consequences.

I thought it should begin with a nurse (Mary Meeks), include a draft resister (Bruce Beyer), Infoage Science and History Museum (Harry Klancer), a novelist who had written about war (David Means-Hystopia), and a poet, writer and veteran (W.D. Ehrhart).

Although I didn't know it when I first contacted Mary, she shares a kind of kinship with Vera Brittain, whose memoir *Testament of Youth* is one of the most important anti-war memoirs ever written and details her own volunteering as a nurse during World War I. Like Vera Brittain, Mary also volunteered to serve in war (Vietnam) after her brother had enlisted in the Marines. Although her brother was never sent overseas, Mary was sent to Vietnam, joining the Army Nurse Corps in 1968, and she worked in the intensive care units of the 3rd Field Hospital in Saigon and the 71st Evac Hospital in Pleiku. I thought a woman's perspective on the human cost of war would be a good beginning to our series.

Her story was the most compelling of all the speakers. Her honest and direct way of speaking, and her clear recollection of the details, brought us all into the hospitals where she was the oldest nurse there at 23 years old.

As Mary remembered some of the soldiers she treated in those hospitals, many in the audience were in tears, including the person filming the event and the local Veterans Service Officer, also a veteran and former helicopter pilot, students and faculty as well. In her short 30-minute talk, she gave her audience the dying moments of both officers and enlisted men she saw die in her intensive care units. Men she could not save. And in her honest description, for a few moments their deaths from serious wounds came into sharp focus and no one could turn away. The nature of the war in Vietnam was there again—painful, bare, uncut. You can hear Mary's own voice online in a variety of formats if you care to listen. She knows those who take care of the wounded see the real tragedy of war.

~ ~ ~

It's Not Unusual

Listen, nothing's easy—you think that and you are gone.
When Mike Woods died of heatstroke no one could believe it; on that one operation alone the Marines lost 60 men from the hot weather and the humidity. Woods and the two guys from our outfit were just three out of the whole lot. Just three. And Robbins, the fourth guy, who came back alive and got to tell the story—how hot it was in those days of April, how they should have been okay by then, they'd been in country for almost six months. They were just there to help those grunts from a line company. Robbins said the heat was too

Epilogue

much, too thick with humidity, too hard to deal with and keep going and guys started to drop even before they'd made contact. It was eerie he said, like you were floating and then falling.

He fell twice himself before a corpsman hit him up with salt tabs and a lot of water. Sitting there in the saddle of a hill, Robbins said he'd seen his whole life flicker like some old newsreel... "I was seeing shit, you dig, I was seeing my own past—my days in high school and even before like I was in the movie and watching it. And I was seeing Smith and Ransom and Woods go down. A haze seemed to be over everything and then the doc calling my name and making me sit down."

They gave him a week in base camp and two days at China Beach. But when Robbins came back, he was still shaken and sometimes when he'd pass by, he seemed as if he were sleepwalking.

~ ~ ~

I found out about Freddy D. from Bob Anthony who had just arrived at 1st Division Headquarters—the general's HQ on the hills above our outfit. We met Anthony and another dude from my high school at the only USO show I ever got to see. It was called "Guys and Dolls"—a musical. No Bob Hope and not too many dolls either, but it was free and there was food and sodas. Anthony asked us to give him a ride back to his hootch, and since we had a PC for the gig that day we agreed. In his tent he confessed his MOS was machine gunner, but they'd sent him to Division HQ as a clerk typist and he was looking to get out, go to a line company. The guys who were with me told him to let it go, stay put, take it easy. He was one month in country and didn't know what was up. I had two months left on my tour.

And right as we were leaving, he told me about Freddy. I'd been friends with his younger brother; we'd run track together in high school.

"Dead before he ever hit the ground, you know. Some kind of electric shock and he lost his grip and fell all the way. He was just a radio guy—you know, comm—and they sent him up there to fix a signal wire. Thailand! Can you get it? Safe. Good duty."

Nobody said anything—but we thought about what it must have been like.

Collateral Damage

~ ~ ~

And then there's the day Harding got run over by a dump truck—a truck loaded with scrap metal and engine parts from the motor-pool guys, old oil drums, leaf springs—that was backing up, the driver just doing his thing.

Harding was fooling around in the company yard. It was growing into dusk and the early dinner chow and he wasn't paying attention. Harding was big, too, at least 200 lbs., and he never had a chance. There was nothing to say about Harding, nothing to do. Two corpsmen came with some of the guys from supply and put him on a stretcher. He was 21. Eight months in country.

~ ~ ~

And then PK. First time he went out with the engineer crew in support of a platoon from Bravo Company, 1st Marines. PK man, he was still new—four months in country and a party animal—always had a joke, a laugh, something to set you back. PK volunteered to go with those guys and then some grunt new guy, two weeks in country, shoots him in the back—an accident—the guy's trigger scared, you know, he's sick from the heat and the stuff he's humping and not paying attention, not thinking it's just a routine patrol, going to support the grunts. PK was my main man, a guy who would dance with us at night. I remember his laugh, his smile, the way he shook his head when he told a good joke.

~ ~ ~

Listen, it goes on and on. And no one remembers, no one even gets it. There were those guys from A Company who got killed in their own tent at night—a three-man team of locals slipped into the compound and shot up the tent and almost got away. The lieutenant said the tent was too close to the wire, too close to the perimeter. But that was a cover-up. Somebody blew the guard detail—probably the lieutenant himself since he was always sneaking around instead of doing his job. That's how those guys died—in their cots. And then there was the cover-up. The bullshit. The colonel coming into it. He knew the lieutenant

Epilogue

was cracked, but they weren't going to court martial no lieutenants, no way. So maybe they listed those guys as KIA, who knows?

And then the others too, after I came home, after I was discharged, after all the "military madness" had ebbed and I was drifting in a cloud of stelazine and beer and regret. My first year in college—bad grades, seeing the campus psychologist, listening, worried about money and tuition. Not doing so well with the courses I took, unable to concentrate.

And then Shaw—Bill Shaw crashing his old Corvette into a tree at night. Frankie said Shaw was sober. He did it on purpose. Too much to deal with, too many things piling up and tumbling down. I liked Shaw—he was honest and smart and he had a sense of humor and a way of understanding the complexity of things. We'd been friends for just a few months. He was the first guy I knew who did it after he was home. But then there were others—you know, the longer you pull away from a war, the deeper the deal, the shadows, and time pulling out all its tricks and deceits. Time calling in the debts, the overdue notices.

Dennis Michaels was another story. He hung himself in his parents' home on Church Street in Binghamton. Michaels was just 19, two months back from his time with the Army; he'd done his required two years and he was free. In high school he ran the 100-yard dash, got a scholarship to Albany, and then the draft came and he was called up. Michaels, whose parents moved away afterwards—back downstate to Elmira where they had kin. There was nothing left for them in the Triple Cities.

Michaels, like the others, one whose name will never be on the wall of names.

~ ~ ~

Ponta de Areia

What we did not know. Most of us, but not all, did not know much about Vietnam. We did not know its customs or traditions. We did not know they had fought off invaders for over 1,000 years.

Collateral Damage

Some of us knew the French had been defeated at a place called Dien Bien Phu. But we did not know where that was or its significance. We did not know Vietnam's history or who its people were—what they believed in, what they had fought for and why. We did not understand the language and most of us failed to learn it very well, if at all.

We knew little about their food, and sadly for many of us, we never got to enjoy it. Some of us, like me, never saw their cities or the beauty of the places in those cities. We didn't know our own history very well, and we certainly had never been taught much of theirs. And, in our ignorance, we stumbled over the simplest things. We did not know they learned from observation, not asking questions.

I learned this years later at the same time I began to understand the history and the culture and the many years of struggle they had endured. I began to understand the awful irony of our war—this war that would become our albatross—so that many of us would go forth and become "wedding guests" who grabbed strangers to tell them stories of our past, stories we wished were not our stories at all.

And as we grew older, many of us never learned from our experiences; instead, we were eaten up by anger and grief and a lingering malaise. And many others came home to learn they had brought the war with them, facing the sicknesses that came from the way the war had been waged—Agent Orange, Agent Blue—chemicals and the afterlife of chemicals.

In our anger and its grief, we destroyed ourselves bit by bit—in drink, in drugs, in a failure to understand what we had done, how we had been used as soldiers are always used by the machines of war, by the industry of war, by the corporations of war and the generals, the politicians, the war profiteers.

And often, even our families—our parents and grandparents, our children, our wives—could not understand us, could not fathom what we had become or why and how it was impossible to rid ourselves of the things we learned there, the truths we came to understand about ourselves, what we had not seen or had been too young to see or understand.

Many years later, a Vietnamese woman who had survived and witnessed the war quietly told a friend of mine when he asked her

Epilogue

why our own country had so much violence in it, why we had become such a violent people: *"It is the ghosts of those who you left behind—they are restless—moving, looking for respite and peace, a peace they cannot find."* He didn't ask her any more questions after that; he listened to her speak about her own journey, her family, her beliefs.

I think many of us were not very good listeners. We learned how not to listen, how not to see the Vietnamese, how to look past them. It is difficult to change, to learn, to find a way to grow out of an experience, to come home and understand a terrible mistake was made and confounded by more mistakes and errors of judgment, compounded by lies and corrupt leadership.

When I was 18 and had just arrived at the metal, makeshift runway in Chu Lai, I did not know that the first time a civilian population had been bombed from the air was during the Spanish Civil War. Now, we were bombing the civilians in Vietnam on a regular basis. I didn't know the extent of how many bombs we dropped on Vietnam until many years later.

And during my first few days in country, our outfit was mortared for the first time. I didn't know what a mortar was, and I didn't know what to do. It was night, the sky glowing from explosions, and I didn't understand what was happening. I think many of the boys who went overseas with me were equally ignorant and unaware—too young to see what was really going on and worried about what to do and how to do it.

All this seems redundant now, especially after all the movies about the war, most just bad—inaccurate—always portraying the Vietnamese as if they were from World War II, looking more like Japanese in Japanese uniforms. The films that seemed to me to reflect the truth were two documentaries: *Hearts and Minds* and *The Anderson Platoon*; and in addition, a "comedy" starring Robin Williams called *Good Morning, Vietnam*. At least in these the Vietnamese are real people and portrayed as such.

And in the end, the only Vietnamese I knew well were two workers who were assigned to help me build structures for equipment and assemble "new" portable tents for generators. Their names, they told me, were Frank and Tom, but I know those were names they gave

Collateral Damage

me to make it easier for me. They were good guys, always amazed at how much "stuff" we had and how much of it we threw away. They wanted our leftover corrugated-tin for their own homes in the village—and the HS gunnery sergeant said it was okay to let them take it home. I arranged a drop off at their village which was not far from our base camp in Danang. I have a snapshot of Frank and Tom next to a pop-up tent that they thought was funny; they could not believe this tent had been sent to us. And I have another photograph of LCpl Keith with a group of Vietnamese boys from the same village; boys Keith was teaching to play basketball.

Later I learned new things about what happened to those who served in Vietnam. I learned the military has its own rules. They try to show you what you are not ... especially if you break the code like I did. There is a payback. It comes with bad paper, or what I got in 1968: a "General Discharge." According to Paul Starr in his book, *The Discarded Army: Veterans After Vietnam*: "During the years of the Vietnam War, the military gave over 200,000 General Discharges,

Danang, 1967. Two Vietnamese brothers, Frank and Tom, with a strange new collapsible tent for equipment.

Epilogue

Danang, 1967. Two Vietnamese brothers/workers.

3% of the discharge total." And in addition, it issued "175,000 Undesirable, Bad Conduct, or Dishonorable Discharges" (pp. 168–169).

What does this mean to the average veteran? It means it's a way to keep you shut down, to humiliate you, to force you to shut up, feel bad about who you are and what you have done. Here's what I wrote to the VA in 2022. Now 50+ years later, and after four years of therapy at the James A. Peters VA Hospital in Bronx, New York, I have come to realize that the tranquilizers were a stumbling block to my recovery. Now I know I needed therapy and counseling. Now I know the tranquilizer led to other depressants like alcohol and then marijuana. It was a natural steppingstone to alcohol and drugs, to feeling depressed and full of self-loathing. A drug that kept my own psychological problems alive.

In a much larger sense, it also fueled the image I had of myself—the idea that "I can't succeed, I don't have what it takes" and a sense of provisional self-esteem. The corporal who as a Marine organized my entire Combat Engineer Battalion's move from Chu Lai to our new base in Danang, who rode shotgun with drivers on TD-15 forklifts from the Port of Danang through the villages along Highway One to the outskirts of Danang for a few days until all our gear was finally on-site; the 19-year-old who had been a "scavenger" for desperately needed parts for our heavy equipment and had even flown back to Chu Lai on a C-130 to "requisition" those wheel cylinders and brake shoes we needed, and all the other war episodes—well, that guy was gone. In his place was a person without confidence and without direction. I felt beaten down, confused and disoriented. In June 1968, I was arrested in Susquehanna, Pennsylvania, and spent the night in jail. Charges were disorderly conduct and suspicious behavior. Pennsylvania State Police arrested me and took me to the local jail where my parents bailed me out the next day and paid the fine. I was twenty. It was less than two months since my discharge.

I Think I'll Call It Morning

The cellar tape. Listen, there's something pulling at me, gnawing at the edge of my dreams, the edge of consciousness. No, it's not a rat—but something unknown, a kind of fear, waves of stuff piling up. The mist comes on with the dusk, and the shadows deepen, and then the dark. It's always when it begins. This is really the state I'm in. I don't tell anyone about it. I'm just aware how those images fill out and become glimpses of things—pieces, fragments.

Like the dream I had as a boy. I'd wake up screaming and sometimes my father would be there shaking me, telling me it was okay. Other times, I'd wake myself up, wondering about the dream—the knights, the clash of lances, the crowds. I could not understand—the jousting, the clash of steel, the cries of the horses, people pushing in on me, crushing me. I never found an answer to the dream. I'd never seen a film about knights. I was too young, second grade. And it was the same dream, again and again.

And I see the room again—with the crucifix on the wall, the guardian angel there too. I see the tan color of the walls, the windows that looked out on the fields across the street before the new houses were built. The street of maple trees that hung over the roadway and

Epilogue

cast their own shadows. The sound of the cars passing beneath those trees.

Later, in college, I told my friend Aaron about the second dream—the sense of someone coming outside the room—and the fear of what or who it was both alarming and penetrating, a deep-seated anxiety even after waking up. Aaron told me, *"When you don't wake up, you'll be dead. It's a death dream."* Aaron used to write out passages from Dostoyevsky—just to get the feel of how the writer did it, pen or pencil—he'd write whole sections. He had *to feel* how to sustain it. I don't know what happened to Aaron. He left college after two years and went back home to Long Island. And then one fall I saw he had published two poems in a very prestigious magazine. He disappeared soon after. I can find no trace of him.

Now they come back when I'm alone, and in the dusk those shadows start to materialize. I can see them—glimpse their faces—this legion. Do I tell my doctor at the hospital about them? Nope. Every time I go there in person, in those long hallways, I look for someone I might know—someone who will turn up—look at me. Would anyone recognize me now? How many years have passed? Too many.

Like the old veteran I picked up hitchhiking near Canandaigua, just outside the VA hospital there.

His name was Willard Cook, and he'd had a tracheotomy, so he used a megaphone gadget they call an *electrolarynx*. He couldn't get back home because of the snowstorm, so he asked me to drive him to a liquor store and get cigarettes and a bottle to take back to his room at the hospital. He had close-cropped, short gray hair and said the doctors told him he had 10 years to live, but he said he'd be happy for three or four years more. He wrote me notes in the front seat of the car to make it easier. I couldn't hear his voice through the electrolarynx over the road noise. When I dropped him back at the hospital he asked me to come and visit him the next time I came for a dental appointment. He had a metal leg plate on the side of his leg and told me in his younger years he'd been a jockey at Belmont—how he'd won a Triple Crown race back then before the service.

Pulling away from the hospital, the traffic was slow. Ice jammed the windshield wipers and made it hard to see. It was two days before

Collateral Damage

Thanksgiving, 1975. I remember driving back to my apartment thinking about those friends ticked off like notches on a wall. Where had they gone? So many roads, so many dead-end streets with the long shriek of sirens chasing the night into another dawn. And the old movie theater in the downtown converted into a diner—a place where I bought coffee.

And now I'm remembering when my father asked me if I wanted any books to read. I was in Chu Lai then, the fall monsoon in full swing. And I wrote him back and said—yes, anything by T.S. Eliot. He sent me a copy of *The Wasteland*. And someone stole that thin book out of my hootch—the canvas tent where Gonzalez and I and a few others slept. No one in that hootch would be reading Eliot or poetry of any kind. It was definitely a *Playboy* or *Penthouse* crew. Maybe some officer stole the book when he came in for inspection. It never got returned.

And I wait for those shadows to take shape—to materialize. It was the same way back when they dedicated the memorial in Washington. I was down there on the grass camped out with a few guys. And then it started to rain. At first, a fine mist of rain so we stayed, but then it got worse and we moved up to the hotel barroom where all kinds of people were drinking and smoking cigarettes. Fred knew, he was a Native American from Maine. He could see them, too. There were definitely ghosts in that crowd. I know—you could see them moving in and out—like smoke or a fine dust of ash.

And they are there waiting. They know I have had a life. And I have to join them at some point. I keep trying to tell a few stories, push away from what is there. The glow, the slow tread of the shadows. The wind helps, when the wind picks up the shadows leave. Keats called the wind "the inland sea." He knew. The wind turns up the leaves and they go silver in the light. I can hear the wind in the leaves of the trees out back, watch the leaves moving. There is a kind of peace in this—a quietude. A calming. Sometimes that's all it takes to still the will-o'-the-wisps. The fragments of fear and grief. And now the other dreams come, each one with its own demands. One night my wife Michele woke me from whatever nightmare I'd had—and again I was not certain what had happened, what I had been

Epilogue

struggling against in the dream, but it seemed like a force to be reckoned with, a threat to me and to those I love. Maybe I have to believe certain things do exist outside of the normal. I have to believe in what others might scoff at or push away.

It's like the sarge taking us all out to see that freighter that had run aground near the base camp at Chu Lai. It was stuck there on a sandbar, rolling from side to side in the surf. The sarge made all six of us climb aboard with him. *"C'mon, you guys got to quit being afraid of stuff, you've got to face each day as an adventure."* And that was Sgt. Bethlehem's attitude for sure. He knew. And he kept pushing us not to be afraid, to discover who we were, where we might be going, what we might encounter next. That ship was weird; you could hear the sea water sloshing down below in the empty hull, you could feel the tug of ocean in its wreck.

Why did they leave it there to break apart in the waves? It was empty of its cargo, and as we walked on the tilted decks you could feel the push and pull of waves, and there was a sense of time passing, of change. We knew we'd be getting orders to other outfits. This FLSG-Bravo thing was short-lived. The war itself would change dramatically in the next six months—and even more so after I went back home. The first Tet Offensive was less than a year away. And I knew our battalion would be moving north again. But that first summer and our short time on the deserted ship has stayed with me. *A ghost ship.*

There are so many ghosts. In Savannah I learned they paint the ceilings of their porches light blue to keep away bad spirits—"haints" folks call them. I've painted all our porch overhangs light blue. Yes. I know you can't keep death away, but maybe you can slow it down, put up some obstacles, get the final protective line set up.

I know Adrian Louis and Horace Coleman would agree. But, they are both gone. They'd say, *"You got to do what you can do. Put up a fight."*

I see my younger brother Dennis when we were both young; he's calling from the backyard of our home on West Main, and suddenly we are running side by side, as if together we could outrun the light that keeps spreading out over the lawns, the maples heavy with summer and a haze seems to cling to us, to choke us with its glow, as if we could outrun even the memory itself, the smoke stacks, the VA homes, the vacant lots. As if in some hollow on the cliffs above the river, we could share our lunch and stare off into the early dusk. And then we are running again, past the chicory, past the black-eyed Susans.

We are young and free and strong and our hearts are rising, falling. We are free and believe the road will come out on the other side, and somehow, we will keep rising toward the light. Yes, for a few moments we are alone, together, the two of us, and there is this opening toward love, toward forgiveness.

~ ~ ~

Today, I think it must have been someone else who waved and walked away—someone else who reeled with the morning and fell asleep finally by the lake. How many nights can someone struggle with the dark, with his own regret? How can he be renewed again? Time rushing past us like the fall wind, like the leaves swirling in circles on the street, the sound of leaves making me remember the fires along the street, the piles of leaves burning in the sunset. And then it's just another fall with the dark coming on early and the cold, swift dusk pulling at us.

It was sad, the night we borrowed that PC and drove into some village—well, when we got to the place Aubrey looked at me and I looked at him and we just knew. *Like what the smoke were we doing there?* These were good people; a family of Vietnamese offering us a few beers, some food. We took the beer and gave them some paper military currency, almost like apologizing for stumbling into their little store, their home as well, so late at night. Both of us aware we had made a mistake.

And all the way back to the battalion gate, drinking the beer, sharing it with those guys in back who were taking the booby-trap course with Sgt. Brody, everyone could feel it, even those new guys. The wrong side of everything. It's part of the same thing. Our intrusion. Our stupidity. And no wonder it's hard to face up to your own past, your drop-down failures.

Epilogue

    Certainly, there were many failures. My wife has a long list of how I failed to live up to things. She's right. And I remember how once she lived on a street with an island in the middle. In the early summer, the linden trees gave off their sweet scent. I remember the flowers that bloomed on that street, and sometimes I imagined I would drive down that street and see her standing there on the porch with her black hair, and I imagined other places we might go, other roads we could take together. Nothing stays the same, and change comes and with change, regret.

    And I'm still stumbling, walking the dream road out and sometimes almost unable to come back. She doesn't understand, and I don't expect her to understand—she's like five years younger than I am. You know. She wouldn't even believe some of the things I've done, although she believes in the things I have not done or left unfinished.

    I have been listening to the rain, the sound of the rain dripping from the eaves, thinking of her wrist—how small and delicate—like the sparrow's song in this late afternoon rain. Her wrist, strong and yet delicate to have lifted all this loss and longing, to have carried it for so long. And I feel my own hand on her wrist, my hand going around it, feeling its grace, its profound dignity. What am I anyway? Someone lost in the rain on this day in fall? Someone who calls your name in this rain? This rain like a kind of weeping, this stillness in the stand of red oaks. It's not enough to know love keeps changing, a symmetry shaped by surprise, by longing, by regret, by anger and loss.

    All the years come piling on and they are jumbled and disorganized like the room I'm writing in—full of books and tools, paint cans and old pictures. A jumble of stuff that tumbles and spins and feels like my life. I can't make sense of things, of this disorder. Perhaps it's a necessary jumble, a need to feel chaotic? I'm not certain that cuts it. And I keep trying to fight everything off, trying to regroup, establish a claim on reality. Maybe, as the doc said, it's no use. You can't get back that lost time, those years. You can't get your youth back. And there's all the baggage, too. I think the solution is to learn how to speak to people again, to try to communicate, to keep forcing yourself to wake up. You can't give in to the ghosts, to the grief, to the overwhelming sadness. I felt like that when I first started to write about the war, how all of us carry the sadness with us as just an "ordinary pain."

In Rome on the Via Carini, someone had scrawled on the side of a building the words *"la guerra e la droga di stato"* or "war is the drug of the state." And it does not stop, these images of death, these pictures torn from the heart of the world, of anger and loss. And I see an old man sitting at a wooden table, his shirtsleeves rolled up. He tells me I should seize the moment, gesturing with his hands. He tells me not to give up, to push on even in the stark, silent hours when I am the one watching the lights flickering up along the hill, the dark night sky coming on, thinking—*if it were sufficient to love.*

In another November, I helped some friends unload lumber for a barn. It was rough-sawn pine and fir—16- and 20-foot beams ticked with yellow splinters. Conrad laughed and pulled the first lengths out—the damp must of raw wood. Conrad who was an Army medic in Vietnam. We saw how the dew had settled on the stacks. It was midday before we had the truck unloaded. The driver jacked his weight to one leg and pushed some beers at us. The sun had warmed the yard, and overhead we heard the great Canada geese heading southward away from the lake. The day was clearing, cold. The driver said there would be snow by nightfall. I listened to them talking of the barn and imagined the rafters going up, the winch and sagging weight of beams propped into place. Later, walking home along the ridge road, I pulled a tufted splinter from my glove and felt the work in my arms like the farmer said, "You'll feel it later, kid." And looking out across the stubble of fields, I felt the tired, slow ebb of youth give way at last. And years later, sitting at a plain deal table beneath the arbor, I remembered Towle's farm, the late fall we raised a barn before the flurries of the first snow, and I knew at last I was home again in a different place and more than 20 years had passed since the day I'd been discharged.

Larks rise in columns of air, fields stretch out, and a path leads up past shops and markets where earlier figs and apricots filled

Epilogue

the wooden crates. Now the windows are shuttered, dark. Another place comes back, a cemetery on a dirt road, a place where farmers lie beneath gravestones rubbed smooth. Near Groveland Station, a late June afternoon, surrounded by summer fields, I wrote down the names. A cemetery hemmed by apple trees, barbed wire, choke weed, tufts of field grass caught in the fenceposts.

I've lost the notebook, the words too, blurred and gone with the moves. And now it's your hand that lifts me up into this present, the hilltop town fanning out, our sons scrambling up the last stone stairs, until the whole valley lies below us.

Turning to look back over the way we have come, I see the streets again, the sound of our shoes against the stones. Maybe each one of us has a past that lives inside of us, a past we do not know or recognize, although moments we believe we see a haze, a movement; a little cup of joy that spills over, leaving us to wonder about hope, a kind of wind that lifts us from loss and grief.

This is not a war story, although there's a war in it and too many deaths. That's it really. It has taken me all these years and all the deaths until my own infant son died to wake me, to rouse me from that sleepwalking state—that dreamer who was unable to see the very dream, the nightmare really, of all that happened, not just in the war but before and after. Is it too late now, too late to make a resolution to keep on waking up? And how is it I am tied to things I had no business in making, tied to the blundering madness of war? Wordsworth wrote, *"We die, my friend/, Nor we alone, but that which each man loved/ And prized in his peculiar nook of earth/ Dies with him, or is changed; and very soon/ Even of the good is no memorial left."*(*The Excursion*)

There are many things I've left out. Like my father's last painting in watercolor pencil—pastels, a landscape. There's a valley in early spring. There are trees about to blossom, trees that lean over a road, and the road leads up out of the valley. No houses or farms. An emptiness grows on you, with the glow rising in hues of ochre and light blue, as if he knew time has its own language. And somehow spring leaps up, pushing a kind of hope outward. It makes me remember the ring he gave me—the ring my mother gave to him—with the inscription in Italian, *Speranza e Verde*. One of the books my father gave me in my second year of high school was *The Hills Beyond* by Thomas Wolfe. A sentence from the section *God's Lonely Man* stays with me: "I have found the constant, everlasting weather of man's life to be, not love, but loneliness."

~ ~ ~

Morning in America

~ ~ ~

Music/Playlist Credits

Dancing in the Dark—Bruce Springsteen/Sarah Vaughan
Like a Rolling Stone—Bob Dylan
What About Me—Quicksilver Messenger Service
Miles from Nowhere—Cat Stevens
One Fine Day—The Chiffons
Will the Circle Be Unbroken?—The Carter Family
Keep On Pushing—The Impressions
Here, There and Everywhere—The Beatles
New Beginnings—Joe Bonner
Standing in the Shadows of Love—The Four Tops
Sunny—Bobby Hebb
Chain of Fools—Aretha Franklin
Where Do We Go from Here?—The Band
Have You Ever Seen the Rain?—Creedence Clearwater Revival
Darkness, Darkness—The Youngbloods
Who'll Stop the Rain?—Creedence Clearwater Revival
Carry That Weight—The Beatles
Slippin' into Darkness—War
Four Days Gone—Buffalo Springfield
Running on Empty—Jackson Browne
When You Awake—The Band
New Beginnings—Joe Bonner
I Walk the Line—Johnny Cash
I Got Dreams to Remember—Otis Redding
If You Want Me to Stay—Sly and the Family Stone
There's a Hole in the Future—Richie Havens
Goin' Out of My Head—Little Anthony & the Imperials
Song of the Wind—Santana
Catch the Wind—Donovan
My Back Pages—Bob Dylan/The Byrds

Music/Playlist Credits

Ain't Nothing Like the Real Thing—Aretha Franklin
New Beginnings—Joe Bonner
Slippin' into Darkness—War
Working Class Hero—John Lennon
Going Down Slowly—The Pointer Sisters
Be True to Your School—The Beach Boys
Homeward Bound—Simon & Garfunkel
Where Did You Sleep Last Night?—Leadbelly
Sweet Melissa—The Allman Brothers
The Other Side of the Sky—Aretha Franklin
Going in Circles—The Friends of Distinction
A House Is Not a Home—Luther Vandross
Estate—Bruno Martino
Dedicated to You—John Coltrane/Johnny Hartman
Sometimes I Feel Like a Motherless Child—Odetta
Hurt—Johnny Cash/Nine Inch Nails
In a Sentimental Mood—Arthur Blythe
Winter in America—Gil Scott-Heron
(Who Wrote) The Book of Love?—The Monotones
Pavane—Maurice Ravel
Rivers of My Fathers—Gil Scott-Heron
When I'm Gone—Brenda Holloway
Orange Crush—R.E.M.
Can't Take My Eyes Off You—Frankie Valli & the Four Seasons
Eight Miles High—The Byrds
Sam Stone—John Prine
If I Could Only Fly—Blaze Foley
Nature Boy—Nat King Cole
The Runaway—Regret the Hour
Time Has Come Today—The Chambers Brothers
You Made Me So Very Happy—Brenda Holloway
Waltzing Matilda—Tom Waits
It's Not Unusual—Tom Jones
Ponta de Areia—Milton Nascimento
I Think I'll Call It Morning—Gil Scott-Heron
Morning in America—Durand Jones & the Indications

Books: A Short List

- *Black POW*, James A. Daly
- *Memphis Nam Sweden*, Terry Whitmore
- *Captain Blackman*, John A. Williams
  Taken together these three works all capture different aspects of what it was like for Black soldiers in Vietnam. *Captain Blackman* is a history of Black soldiers in all of our wars, told through the lens of a Black officer who has been wounded. Terry Whitmore and James A. Daly have both written what I call "resistance narratives," and they confront what it was like to push back against the military and face the consequences.
- *Busted* and *Vietnam Perkasie*, W.D. Ehrhart. No one is better than Bill Ehrhart at reminding us how and why we failed to understand the war in Vietnam. Read Ehrhart's poems too, especially the collection *To Those Who Have Gone Home Tired*.
- *And a Hard Rain Fell*, John Ketwig. This memoir served as an early inspiration for me, and his honesty cuts both ways.
- *Meditations in Green*, Stephen Wright. This novel really captures many of the aspects of my own time in Vietnam, or what was beginning to happen as the war got even more absurd.
- *Born on the 4th of July*, Ron Kovic. This short and poignant autobiography is told in first and third person as the writer wakes up to his own *Johnny Got His Gun* reality. It was a book that brought me home.
- *Winners & Losers*, Gloria Emerson. Winner of the National Book Award and an unflinching look at the truths behind the generals.
- *In the Grass*, Horace Coleman. For me Horace Coleman's poems have always been a source of personal inspiration; he knew the "darkness" we carried was real.
- *The Short Timers*, Gustav Hasford. Many saw the film *Full Metal Jacket*, yet this short novel is like "being punched six or seven times" and is not *the movie*.

Books

- *De Mojo Blues,* A.R. Flowers. One of the best novels about Vietnam and coming home from the war.
- *The Discarded Army—Veterans After Vietnam,* Paul Starr with James Henry & Raymond Bonner. This book has information about how many Vietnam vets were issued *bad paper* or less than honorable discharges and how this posed serious issues in both employment and veterans benefits.
- *Waiting for an Army to Die,* Fred Wilcox. Get both the first and the revised editions. The most important book about the chemicals we used to defoliate an entire nation, including all those who fought in the "conflict."
- *War and the Soul: Healing Our Nation's Veterans from Post-Traumatic Stress Disorder,* Edward Tick. The real view of PTSD without pulling any punches.
- *Novel Without a Name,* Duong Thu Huong. This novel by a Vietnamese writer and dissident has been left out of required reading lists for too long. It is an unforgettable story.
- *The Sorrow of War,* Bao Ninh. From its opening page, this novel lets the reader see the war many Americans still refuse to understand.
- *Street Without Joy,* Bernard Fall
- *Fire in the Lake,* Francis Fitzgerald
- *After Our War,* John Balaban
- *Going After Cacciato,* Tim O'Brien
- *When Heaven and Earth Changed Places,* Le Ly Hayslip
- *In the Combat Zone—An Oral History of Women in Vietnam,* Kathryn Marshall

Index

Adige River, Italy 193
Adirondacks 195
Agent Blue 215
Agent Orange 167, 215
Albany, New York 17, 20, 27, 74
Alexander, Michelle 175
Alpha Company 6
Alzheimer's 143, 207
American Legion 117
The Anderson Platoon (film) 216
Angola State Prison 171
Anti-Submarine Squadron 136
Appalachian Trail 141
Appia Antica 193
Arlington National Cemetery 165
Armed Forces Radio 11
Army Nurse Corps 211
Arno River 194
Arthur Kill 195
Attica prison 11, 12, 129, 171–174, 177–178, 180, 184–185, 198, 206
Aunt Eleanor 134
AWOL 7, 35, 64, 65, 67, 72, 74, 76, 78, 79, 83, 112

B-29 136
Baldwin, James 171
Bassano del Grappa 192
Bayliff's Bar 78
Be True to Your School 122
Beach Boys 122
Belmont 220
Bethesda, Maryland 23
Bethlehem, Sergeant 45, 49
Beyer, Bruce 160, 169, 210
Binghamton, New York 15, 17, 58, 72, 73, 75, 153, 214
Binghamton University/SUNY Binghamton 148
Bisio, Aldalgisa 144–147
Black Lives Matter 172

Blood and Guts 209
Bloom, Captain 47
Bravo Company, 1st Marines 213
Brenta River, Italy 192
Brittain, Vera 210
Bronx 197
Bronx, VA 35
Bronze Star 27
Brooklyn Brig 18, 71, 78, 82, 112, 205
Brooklyn Navy Yard 70
Brown, James 10
Buddha 102
Buffalo, New York 128
Buffalo Nine 160
Buick Plant 113, 191
Burma 135–137

C-Files VA 101
C-130 54, 219
Calamandrei, Antonio 152
Calcutta, India 136
Cambodia 6, 56
Camilo Mejia 64
Camp Hansen 19
Camp Lejeune 29, 30, 105
Camp Pendleton 105
Canandaigua, New York 15, 220
Canon camera 72
Captain Marvel 88
Caravaggio(s) 194
Caterpillar Pin/Club 137
Cedar River-Iowa 124
Charleston, South Carolina 65, 66, 72
Charlotte, North Carolina 21
Chemung 191
Chenango 191
Chevrolet Impala 71
Chianti 140
chief of police 62
Chimney Mountain 195
China 137

233

Index

China Beach 60
Chu Lai 18, 34, 41, 54, 55, 72, 75, 130, 131, 164, 166, 178, 219, 221, 222
Cimino 202
Clinton Correctional Facility 184
Coca-Cola girls 6
Coleman, Horace 8, 222
Conover, Ted 179
Constitution Avenue 168
Constitution Hall 164
contraband 184
Convicted Voices 184
Cook, Willard 220
Cooper, Gary 90
Cortland 15
Corvette 214

Dannemora 184
DAR 164
Davis, Angela 174
Davis, Miles 11
DD 553 64
DDT 38
Death Row 184
The Deer Hunter 200, 201
Delaware 71
Delaware River 207
DeNiro 202
Deposit, New York 31
Dillard, Lawrence Ike 184
Dingbat Lee 94
Disneyland 22
The Divine Comedy 148
DMZ 56, 202
Doctor Morley 80, 109, 203
Doctor Spencer 92, 109
Dodge Dart 180
Dominican Republic 204
Don and Bob's 163
Dostoyevsky 220
Douglass, Frederick 174, 182
DPW 200
Drifters 7
Dylan, Bob 14

East River 192, 195
Eddie's Radiator Repair 144
Ehrhart, W.D. 210
EJ (Endicott Johnson)Shoe Factories 114
El Toro, California 58
electrolarynx 220
Eliot, T.S. (*The Wasteland*) 221
Elizabethan Drama 129

Emerson, Gloria 160–163
Endicott, New York 15
Engineer Battalion, 1st Combat 47
Erie Lackawanna Line 31

FBI 64
Finger Lakes 115
Firenze (Italy) 194
First Division Headquarters (1st) 212
First Marine Headquarters 54
Fitzpatrick, Martin 184
Flaubert, Gustave 126
Flint, Michigan 113
Floyd, George 172
FLSG-Bravo 47, 48, 51, 222
Flushing River 195
La Fontana di la Tortugas 193
Ford Galaxy 68
France 139
French Church (Rome) 194
Freshman Composition 129

Galutz, Jim 23
"General Discharge" 217
Geneseo, New York 128
Genoa, Italy 145
Giant Market 75
Gibbons, Reginald 162
Gilder Lehrman Center for American History 210
Good Morning, Vietnam (film) 216
Greene, New York 17
Greyhound Bus 17
Griggs, Brent I. 18, 19, 40, 84
Guys and Dolls 212

Hales Eddy, New York 31
Harpur College 148
Harvey 83
Hatton, Bill 208
Hearts and Minds (film) 216
Hell's Kitchen 90, 135, 137
Hernandez, Miguel 184
Heron, Gil Scott 162, 171, 177
Highway One 7, 48, 50
Hilltop Farm 195
Ho Chi Minh 47
Hofman, Paul 193
Hook Mountain 195
Hope, Bob 212
Hospital Audiences Incorporated 178
Hudson River 195
Hue, Hue City 205
La Huerta Press 185

234

Index

Hughes, Langston 192
Hunter College, New York City 148

IBM 33, 140, 148
Ichabod 18
India 139
Infoage Science and History Museum 210
Inside: Writing by Attica Inmates 184
Inwood, New York City 134
Iowa City, Iowa 125
Iraq War 199
Irish, Jane 208
ITR 18

Jackson, George 175
Jacobs, Harriet 174
James E. Strates Shows 121
JFK Airport 58
Johnson City, New York 153
Jones, James 69

Kafka 171
King, Martin Luther 11, 70, 112
King's Flow 195
Klancer, Harry
Korea 27
Korean Marine 60
Korean War 48
Kramer, Sarah, NPR 174

Lake Ontario, New York State 116, 130
Lakeville, New York 177
Lakota 163
Laramie, Wyoming 125
Last Parallel 27
Letting Go (novel by Philip Roth) 71
leukemia 200
Library of America 210
Lifton, Robert 161
Ligurian seacoast, Italy 145
Lin, Maya 162
Little Anthony and the Imperials 94
Little League 89, 90
Livingston County, New York 128
Lollobrigida, Gina 193
Long Binh Jail 174
Louis, Adrian 222
Lucca, Italy 146
lymphoma 200

M1-rifles 28
M-16 (rifle) 6
M-79 166

Malcolm X 174
Manhattan 195
Marine Air Station, Cherry Point, North Carolina 32, 53, 105
Marine Barracks, Sea School 65, 72, 82, 205
Marine Reserve Station 68
Mastro, Guidice 148
Mead, South Dakota 165
Means, David (Hystopia) 210
Meeks, Mary Edie 210
Milton, Staff Sergeant 45
Mohawk Airlines 21–22, 70
Monkees 104
MOS (military occupational specialty) 212
Mule, Military M274 Truck 51
Mustapha 177

Nanticoke Creek 113, 122, 135, 191
National Catholic Reporter 162
National Defense Ribbon 30
National Endowment for the Humanities 210
Native Americans 103
Naval Weapons Station 66
Neuro Psychiatric Unit 112, 205
New Delhi, India 136
New Jack 179
New York State Council on the Arts 206
New York Times 35, 162
Newark, New Jersey 112
Norfolk, Virginia 66, 70, 71, 82, 103, 112
North Carolina 197
NSU 6

Odysseus 186
Office of Volunteer Services 178
Okinawa 9, 19, 40, 58, 60, 84, 105, 123
Old Gold cigarettes 79
On the Road 77
Onondaga County Jail 68, 78, 112
Operation Iraqi Freedom 199
Operation Union II 7, 38
Oppen, George 173
Otsego 191
Ozymandias 171

Park Lane Boulevard 6
Parris Island 21, 22, 23, 105, 177
Pavese, Cesare 57, 150
PC (personnel carrier) 212
Peace Bridge, Buffalo, New York 160
pedophile 207

235

Index

Pennsylvania State Police 219
Penthouse 221
Peters, James A. Veterans Hospital 219
Philadelphia, Pennsylvania 87
Phoebe Snow (train) 31
Piazza Mattei 193
Pilgrim, Billy 35
Pine, Courtney 192
ping-pong 88, 94–95
Pittsford, New York 163
Playboy 221
Pleiku, Vietnam 211
Poets & Writers 206
Poets in the Schools Program 129
POM Juice 6, 54
Ponte Sisto 192
Ponte Vecchio 194
Pontiac Catalina 125
Porta Portese (Rome)
Porter, Gareth 162
Portsmouth, Virginia 205
Portsmouth Brig 82
Powers, Kevin 35
President's Own 67
Protestant Cemetery (Rome) 194
PTSD 35, 109
Puglia, Italy 148

Quaker Lake, Pennsylvania 31
Queens 195
quonset hut 60

Reader's Digest 88
Recco, Italy 145
Richmond Creek 195
Robbins, Tom 175
Rochester, New York 61
Rochester Institute of Technology (RIT) 61
Roethke, Theodore 195
Rome, Italy 191, 193–194, 225
RPGs 199
Russ, Martin 27
Russian Roulette 201

Saigon 9, 211
Saint Albans Hospital 79
Sale, Roger 175
San Casiano in Val de Pesa, Italy 145–146
Sanchez, Sonia 11, 175
Savannah, Georgia 222
Scranton, Pennsylvania 72, 114
Seneca Lake, New York 144

Seneca's Tomb 193
Seventy First Evac Hospital (71st) 211
Shenandoah song by Odetta 126
Silone, Ignazio 140
Silver Lake, Pennsylvania
Sketches of Spain 11
Slaughterhouse-Five or The Children's Crusade 35
slow-downs 184
South Carolina 20
South China Sea 51
Special Training Battalion (STB) 26
Starr, Paul 217
Starrucca, Pennsylvania 31
State Park Police 128
State Radio/Dispatch 64
State University of New York at Geneseo 114
Stelazine 79, 82, 203
Superman 88
Susquehanna, Pennsylvania 31, 206, 219
Susquehanna River, New York State 113, 135, 191
Swatara 191
Syracuse, New York 68, 205

Tam Ky 51
Tarawa 139
TD-15 (Forklift) 17
Temptations 9
Tennessee 181
Tet Offensive 11, 102, 205, 222
Texaco Station 125, 127
Thailand 38, 212
Third Field Hospital (3rd) 211
Thompson, Heather Ann 176
Thorazine 107
Tiber River, Rome 192, 194
Title 1 ESEA 183, 201
Tokyo 58
Tom's River, New Jersey 207
Trailways 21, 58, 184
trigger squeeze 24
Trim a Tree 76
Triple Cities College 148
Triple Cities, New York State 112, 214
Troy, Doris 7
Trust, Dougson 129
Tuscany 140
Twentieth Air Force (20th) 136

Ugino, John Joseph 164

Variety Inn 206

236

Index

Varysburg, New York State 128
Veterans Day Parade 1982 162
Veterans Service Officer 211
Via Carini (Rome) 225
Via Ripetta (Rome) 194
Viet Cong 52, 107
Vietnam Brotherhood Association 164
Vietnam Veterans Against the War (VVAW) 160
Vietnam Veterans Memorial 162
Vonnegut, Kurt 35

wailing wall 165
Walter Reed Hospital 87, 107
Ward 13 85, 94, 103
Washington Hotel 167
Washington Monument 168
Watkins Glen, New York 148
Wayne, John 90, 202

Weinberger, Caspar 165
West Endicott, New York 151
West Virginia drawl 93
Wicker, Tom 175
Williams, Robin 216
Wilson, Nancy 46
Winter Soldier Investigation 49, 208
Wolfe, Thomas (*The Hills Beyond*; *God's Lonely Man*) 227
Woodlawn Cemetery 145
Wordsworth, William 226
World War I 210
Wright, James 193
Writers Workshop, University of Iowa 124
Wyoming County, New York 171

Yellowcake 199

www.ingramcontent.com/pod-product-compliance
Ingram Content Group UK Ltd.
Pitfield, Milton Keynes, MK11 3LW, UK
UKHW041940140426
5217IPUK00014B/573